x

Beginning
Well

"Joel Stepanek has done an immense service in *Beginning Well*. Offering a combination of professional skills and life experience—illumined by the Catholic faith—Stepanek helps young professionals (or anybody starting something new) navigate transitions in life. Through everything from overcoming imposter syndrome to the necessity of finding a mentor, Stepanek offers a plan for peace and confidence. If you want advice and coaching that combine faith and serious practical know-how, this is the book for you!"

Andrew D. Swafford
Associate professor of theology at Benedictine College

"Joel Stepanek gives a clear and captivating message: Beginnings are a gift and knowing the Lord as you pursue new things is the way to succeed. I not only enjoyed this book but I also found it to be a source of inspiration and encouragement. Don't hesitate to read this book and pass it along. It's full of good advice, necessary tips, and timeless wisdom."

Katie Prejean McGrady
Host of the *Ave Explores* podcast and
The Katie McGrady Show on SiriusXM

Beginning Well

7 Spiritual Practices for the First Year of Almost Anything

Joel Stepanek

AVE MARIA PRESS AVE Notre Dame, Indiana

© 2021 by Joel Stepanek

Founded in 1865, Ave Maria Press is a ministry of the United States Province of Holy Cross.

www.avemariapress.com

Paperback: ISBN-13 978-1-64680-135-0

E-book: ISBN-13 978-1-64680-136-7

Cover and text design by Andy Wagoner.

Printed and bound in the United States of America.

Library of Congress Cataloging-in-Publication Data is available.

———✕———

For Colleen, in gratitude
for all the beginnings we've shared
and all the beginnings we've yet to experience.

———✕———

Contents

Introduction

My heart raced with excitement and anxiety. My feet were heavy as I stepped toward the unknown. I knew that after this coming year was over, I was going to be different, but I had no idea how that would happen or what I would be like once the year was done. I only knew that life was going to change. I stepped up and onto the bus for my first day of kindergarten and never looked back!

Some beginnings stick with us in memory. Maybe for you it was your first day of high school or college. It might have been the first day on your first real job. You might have vivid memories of the first day after your marriage or the day after your first child was born. I remember the first day after my son was born, but the next six weeks are a blur.

Beginnings happen for us more often than we realize because beginnings aren't always firsts. Parenting my first child, Elijah, was a wild adventure. In the first few years of his life, alongside my wife, I learned a lot, faced new challenges, and experienced a lot of joy. When we had my daughter, Sophia, it was just as much of an adventure. It wasn't a first, but it was a beginning. We begin things all of the time.

We begin when we decide to go on that diet, start a new job, get sober, go back to school, or walk away from an unhealthy relationship. Sometimes beginnings aren't our choice but rather the result of circumstances beyond our control. We have a new beginning when we bury a loved one or when we lose our jobs.

Regardless of how they come about, our beginnings present opportunities to transform us for better or for worse. What that change looks like is determined by how we embrace and navigate them.

I recently finished my first year of a new job after having been promoted to an executive position at my organization. That was an exciting day; I felt like my hard work leading teams, directing projects, and developing my staff were recognized and affirmed. I texted my wife the news before I drove home, and by the time I got there she had poured a couple of glasses of my favorite bourbon to celebrate. As I raised the glass, a sudden, dreadful feeling came over me. My wife asked what was wrong. I said, "I feel like I'm looking into a dark tunnel and have no idea what is on the other side or if a train is going to come and hit me." My wife stared at me quietly for a moment, then raised her glass and proposed a toast, "Here's to being daring enough to risk the train."

Beginning something new is scary because there are many unknowns. I began my first year as an executive in September 2019, and six months later the COVID-19 pandemic hit. It wasn't exactly like being hit by a train, but like being smashed by a rocket ship. I felt like every day I walked into the office was a new start because I had no idea what was coming next.

I could look back and say that first year was terrible, and not the kind of *terrible* we use to describe poor service at a restaurant when we write a scathing review on Yelp. It was the kind of terrible that can leave you broken, beat up, and scarred, never wanting to begin again. But instead, I believe that new beginning made me resilient, empowered, and strong. When we face the oncoming train, we can choose how we move. I navigated my beginning with a set of tools that I had built up from my many first years, fresh starts, and new adventures. Our beginnings—no matter what they are—follow a pattern and include similar obstacles, opportunities, and chances to correct course.

This pattern exists in your new job and in your first year of marriage. It exists in the first year of life after your first child is born and the first year of life after your seventh child is born. It is the same pattern that happens in a voluntary first year, such as when we start a new exercise routine or move to a new city, or involuntarily, such as when we lose a job or a loved one passes away. There are practical things we can do to make transitions positive growth experiences, to help us begin well.

But that's only part of it. There is a spiritual component that accompanies the practical. If we lean into our beginnings and recognize the ways God is present in every moment, journeying with us, we can be transformed emotionally, physically, and spiritually.

The Great Metanoia

There is a word for this kind of journey—*metanoia*. The word means "to go another way" or "to go a new way." The early Christian community used this word to describe the spiritual journey one undertook when they began following Jesus. I like the word for beginnings because it captures the deeper reality of a new start.

Unfortunately, we often don't focus on the spiritual aspect of new things because we get so caught up in trying to do the practical well. We end up feeling as though we barely have time to get our feet underneath us in our new endeavor, let alone look at how we may be able to spiritually grow. But we can do both and do both well. We just need to be intentional about it.

It isn't an easy path, but it is a simple one. We often complicate things that don't need to be and then make excuses to not do them. This book is about simplicity in growth. But there is danger in simplicity. Simple things, repeated over time, become skills; simplicity is not something we can do quickly, last minute, or without intention. Simple is not always easy.

If you're already midway through your beginning, it isn't too late. You may be a few months into the job, marriage, school, or fitness routine and find yourself overwhelmed at this new thing you started. You may already be a year in, wondering how to pivot to get back on track. The beauty of metanoia is that it begins with a decision to change course. There is no predetermined time frame to make that decision—you can make it anytime. If you've been at something for a while, however, there may be some habits or practices you've set up that need to be undone. Keep in mind that beginnings can happen in middles.

Using This Book

This book is meant for anyone who is beginning something, and it is designed for both spiritual and practical growth. Each chapter is broken into four sections that follow the same simple template. Beginnings can be overwhelming, and my goal in each chapter is simplicity so you can grab hold of each concept and apply it to your particular circumstance.

In the first section, the challenge and opportunity of a new beginning is laid out along with a habit for how we can begin well. There are seven of these habits: looking forward rather than back, leveraging a skills toolbox, asking good questions, creating rituals, evaluation and reflection, finding mentors, and embracing joy.

The second section of each chapter offers a scriptural narrative to help ground each concept in our faith. Beginnings are human experiences, and the Bible is filled with human experiences. What makes the Bible so incredible is that it offers insight into how God is a part of our human experiences.

The third section offers spiritual insight into each habit. Remember, our beginnings are moments for metanoia and provide opportunities for us to grow spiritually. These spiritual habits can be applied any time in our lives, but are especially relevant when we are beginning something new.

The fourth section of each chapter provides practical insights and exercises for how to begin well. God wants us to be holy, and holiness means living an integrated life. God does not want you to fail at your new endeavor. God wants you to begin well. Don't skip over the practical pieces or exercises. They are here to help make your new beginning an opportunity for growth and success.

Jesus Take the Train

It can be unnerving to stare down the dark tunnel of a new beginning and see the work that is necessary to make it something transformative. There is a particular story about Jesus inviting people to beginnings that I love because it captures the fear and hope we experience when opportunity calls.

Jesus is teaching from a boat that some fishermen own. Afterward, he asks to go fishing. The fishermen, however, have been trying to catch fish for several hours prior and haven't been successful. They are cleaning their equipment, and putting their nets back in the water will undo all that work. As if the audacity of the request, given the circumstances, wasn't enough, the timing wasn't at all good for fishing. Still, they oblige the request and catch an unexpected amount of fish. Something incredible has happened, but now there is a choice.

Peter, one of the fishermen, is overwhelmed at what happened and is happening, so much so that he asks Jesus to leave. His exact words are, "Depart from me, for I am a sinful man, O Lord" (Lk 5:8). Jesus works a miracle, and Peter feels unworthy. Then Jesus invites Peter to a beginning, and Peter needs to make a choice. Peter can hang on to what has been and who he was—a self-proclaimed sinful man—or he can start something new, something he hasn't done before. Perhaps it is the next words of Jesus that give Peter the encouragement he needs. Looking at Peter kneeling at his feet, Jesus responds, "Do not be afraid" (Lk 5:10). Then Peter follows Jesus.

Beginnings are like that. Sometimes beginnings are expected, and other times they seem to come out of nowhere. Whether planned or impromptu, Jesus is in our beginnings and helps us begin well. Peter stepped off the boat to follow Jesus, and he would never be the same. You can step into something new at this moment, in a unique but no less powerful way, as you hold this book. Jesus is waiting for you to leave the old nets behind and start off on something new. Let's begin.

1 Let Go of What You Left

We were excited but nervous. I had lived in Wisconsin my entire life and my wife, besides the two years she lived in Wisconsin, had lived in Philadelphia her whole life. That morning we got into our tiny car, packed tight with our belongings, and moved from Wisconsin to Arizona, driving across the country into a new frontier.

When you drive west in the United States, you notice how the landscape subtly changes. At a certain point, the colors shift from a palate of greens, blues, and yellows to browns, deep reds, and the pale green color of plants that have adapted to harsher environments. The landscape isn't all that changes—the architecture changes, the kinds of fast food chains you see shifts, and even the rules are different. (Did you know there are highways on which you can drive as fast as 85 miles per hour in Texas?) When you move, the transition from what was to what will be can be a visual experience as well as an emotional one. The emotional piece is where my wife was during the ride.

She talked about how she didn't like the cactuses and commented on the lack of trees. She remarked that the houses didn't feel the same and she didn't like the style. I felt all the same things. This was something new in a lot of ways, and it seemed the only reminders of home were the Starbucks coffee shops we stopped at on our way.

When we finally arrived in Phoenix after the three-day journey, we stopped to pick up supplies at a Target store. As my wife got out of the car, I spilled coffee all over her white shirt, and emotions boiled over. She broke down in tears, saying, "I hate this place, I want to go home." I felt a knot in my stomach. In that moment, going home felt like a good choice.

For the next few months we tried to look for the good things in our new place, but it never felt like home. We spent our time talking about how we missed the places we used to go out to dinner, our friends back home, and the church we attended. Even some of the things we didn't like so much about our old town we suddenly found endearing. We got very sad after those conversations, longing to go home and escape our current situation.

We had almost gotten through a year when I asked my bosses if I could work remotely from Wisconsin.

They reluctantly agreed to try it out with the caveat that they could call at any time for me to return to the office in Phoenix. When I told my wife the news, we were so happy. We began to make plans for all the things we would do when we moved back. A couple of months later, we packed up our tiny car and drove east, looking out the windows as browns and reds gave way to greens and blues.

Beginnings in Scripture

There is a story in the Bible about a man named Lot and his family. They live in a town that is filled with some particularly vicious people. The people of this town are so vicious, in fact, that when visitors come to Lot's family, the men of the town threaten to sexually assault them as a sign of dominance, power, and humiliation. This is horrific because sexual assault is absolutely evil and, in this case, the evil is compounded because these visitors are divinely appointed messengers. They've come to check out how bad this town is and are there to deliver bad news: God has decided that this particular place needs to be wiped off the map, and Lot's family, the only good people in the town, needs to leave immediately.

There are many layers to this story. It is a narrative that can raise a lot of questions. Many people debate the exact reason why God chose to destroy this town. Some people take issue with the fact that God is depicted as choosing to destroy an entire town of people in a divine display of capital punishment. There are scholars who focus on a dialogue Abraham has with God during which Abraham argues that the town should not be destroyed if there are even a few righteous people still in it and, through a back and forth bargain, God agrees that if there are as few as ten good people there, he will not destroy the city. These scholars wonder whether this means God changes his mind or if God is just humoring Abraham. If you ever read more about this story or hear someone talk about it, you may hear some of these questions.

They are good questions and discussions, but they don't tell us much about beginnings. One character does, though, and I'm fascinated with her story.

Lot's Wife and the Good Ol' Days

Despite Abraham's bargaining with God, it turns out that God isn't able to find even ten righteous people in this town except for Lot's family. God sends a message to Lot to leave the town before it is destroyed and includes one minor but important detail: Do not look back.

That shouldn't be too hard. This town is filled with so many people who are violently inhospitable that the town isn't worth saving. This town seems like a place Lot should have left years ago. But beginnings aren't always that easy, and this seems especially so for Lot's wife.

Although the town that Lot and his family are fleeing isn't a good place, it's still home. Lot's wife is feeling that as she walks away. Perhaps she is thinking of friends she had there who, while not the greatest people, were still friends. She may have been thinking about her home and the memories the family made there or events that happened in the community. Sure, there were things that weren't good but she isn't thinking about them now. She is remembering the good things.

Distance always seems to round out the rough edges, though. As we get further away from something it is as though the bad memories fade from our view and the good ones shine even brighter. We all do this, even when we leave something bad.

We think about how good he was to us on our anniversary, even though we know we left because he was toxic. We remember the time we landed the big account with our team, even though we know that later our boss took all the credit for it. We look back at high school, or college, or graduate school, wanting to go back but forgetting how we couldn't wait to graduate.

In those moments, we want to look back, but not to steal a glance. We want to look back because we want to *go* back. That's why the glance backward is dangerous. If we stop and turn around we will only see what was good and, if we aren't careful, we may find ourselves going back the way we came. There are moments when we need to keep our eyes forward and let go.

This is especially difficult in involuntary beginnings. Leaving a bad situation makes it easier to focus on the future, but when our beginning is the result of an ending we didn't choose, such as a layoff, forced move, death, or divorce, we may struggle to keep our eyes forward. In these moments it is important to work with people, whether they are family, friends, or counselors, who can help us keep focused on the future as we let go of the past. Trauma from a bad ending can keep us stuck for a long time, fearful to move on because we don't want to forget what we lost. We need people who can keep our eyes forward.

Lot's wife, unfortunately, can't help herself. As she walks away, the sound of the the town where she lived being destroyed catches her attention and she turns back to get one last look—and she immediately wishes she hadn't done that. Her backward glance is her last. Lot's wife remains forever locked into a final gaze with the city she left as she is turned into a pillar of salt. Debates about the narrative aside, the lesson here is certain: Looking back longingly at our past—especially if that past wasn't as good as we think it was after a little distance distorts our memories—can prove devastating.

My wife and I moved back to Wisconsin in August, which is a great time of the year to be in Wisconsin. We did all the things we wanted to do: we ate at our favorite restaurants, saw old friends, and got an apartment twice as big with rent half as much as our apartment in Phoenix. We felt great about our move.

But just as distance can round out the rough edges of our memories, getting close can uncover those edges again. There were things we didn't like but had forgotten—not the least of which was the two months of subzero temperatures during our winter back. We misjudged what the community would look like when we returned. It had changed since we left, and we had changed, too. After the first few months home, unsettled feelings returned, and we remembered some of the reasons we were excited to move to Arizona. We loved living in Wisconsin, but the return wasn't what we thought it would be. After a year in Wisconsin, my boss called me and offered a new position and a move back to Arizona. After a few weeks of discernment, my wife and I left Wisconsin again and returned to the desert.

Spiritual Beginnings

I've onboarded staff members into teams for over a decade, and I've learned to identify early the people who will make it in a new role and those who will struggle in their first year (many of whom will move on). The people who do well in new roles share a particular outlook, which dramatically changes their new beginning. Those who were successful in their first year had a funeral for whatever they left behind. Every one of them who failed their first year had tried to resurrect the dead.

Whenever we experience loss we go through a period of grieving. This period of time is important because it allows us to process our loss and move on. Many people fail to grieve, though, because they are afraid to let go. They want to look back at what has been rather than moving on. If we stay stuck in the past we miss the new things that are beginning and the great opportunities they present.

There is a spiritual component to this that is rooted in the most profound beginning of history. When Jesus died on the Cross, it seemed like an ending—a horrific and unexpected ending. The followers and friends of Jesus believed that the story was over, but they were wrong. Something new began with the death of Jesus. Without that death, there would be no Resurrection.

To put it into one of my love languages—'90s pop music—"every new beginning comes from some other beginning's end" (and long before Semisonic sang it in "Closing Time," the Roman Stoic philosopher Seneca said it). Dying and rising is foundational to the Christian life and has implications for us beyond succeeding at a new beginning. God can do great things through the deaths we experience, but we need to be looking for resurrection rather than staring blankly at the cross.

The Cross, Grave, Empty Tomb, and Irish Wakes

Lot's wife wasn't the only person in the Bible who had a problem with looking backward. After Jesus dies and is placed in the tomb, there are a couple of people who struggle with looking backward. The first is Mary

Magdalene. She goes to the tomb of Jesus and finds it empty. She is distressed, believing that robbers took the body. Suddenly, Jesus is standing with her. There is a curious detail about this story. Mary doesn't realize it is Jesus and believes he is the gardener for that area. Jesus reveals himself to her, and Mary exclaims excitedly, "Teacher!" She runs to Jesus, but Jesus tells her to "not hold" him. Is Jesus just not a hugging person? This goes much deeper than physical affection.

Mary doesn't recognize Jesus because she is looking backward and, even when Jesus reveals himself, Mary still calls Jesus "Teacher" rather than Messiah or Lord. She remembers who Jesus was, or who she thought he was, as a rabbi. She was looking backward, and it prevented her from seeing the Resurrection right in front of her.

The same thing happens to two of Jesus's disciples after the burial. They are returning to their home city when Jesus begins walking with them. Again, they don't recognize Jesus right away. Instead, they tell Jesus (who they think is a new travel companion) all about the ending. Jesus helps correct their vision and, eventually, reveals himself to them.

We do this, too. We get focused on endings and fail to see new beginnings. This is especially challenging when our ending feels a lot more like a death. There are exciting beginnings that come from endings, such as starting a job we are excited about, marriage, starting college, or moving out on our own. It's still important to grieve for those endings, but easier to look ahead. When we encounter an involuntary ending, though, that feels a lot like a cross; we can easily get locked into a gaze backward, stuck in grief.

The death and Resurrection of Christ point to something big in our spiritual life. Every death brings about resurrection when we invite Jesus into that moment. This is true for happy endings and sad endings. Death leads to resurrection as the gateway to something new in our spiritual lives. If we can adopt this mindset, we begin to embrace the moments of death and ending in our lives and open ourselves up to the new work God can do through them. When we lose a job, we can earnestly pray and say, "Lord, bring about new life in this moment." Then we can look.

This isn't an easy mindset. We can look to the Cross and embrace the theory of it as a spiritual practice, but in practical terms, this is challenging. We need a new approach to death and grief in order to really make the paradigm shift. A model exists in the Irish wake for a grief that embraces death while looking ahead to resurrection. The Irish wake is a tradition that mirrors aspects of what we understand a wake to be, but the tone of the event is more celebratory. The deceased is celebrated with stories various family members share. Each person gets a special, final moment with the loved one over the course of a couple of days. It is a way of grieving that accepts the finality of death while celebrating what was and what is becoming. That part is crucial—themes of resurrection and peaceful departure are present in a traditional Irish wake. There is something to be mourned in the loss of a life, yet something to be celebrated.

This mindset becomes a life vest in our first year of almost anything. If we can let go of what was, we can embrace what is becoming.

When we begin something new, the tendency, especially if we haven't grieved for what we've left behind, is to put the new into the context of the old. We think by comparison about our new job in terms of the old job, the new town in terms of the old town, the new relationship in terms of the old relationship. That kind of thought is limiting because we find ourselves continually talking about the way it was or how things turned out last time. We look backward.

Grieving turns our heads forward at the right time. When we lay what has passed to rest, we free our hands to take hold of what is coming into being. There is a reason we throw bachelor and bachelorette parties, even if we've lost that meaning culturally. There is a reason people go out to have one last unhealthy meal before they start a diet. There is a reason we throw goodbye parties at work and why we cry when we leave our office for the last time. We need to do that in order to move on or we risk looking back and losing everything.

Beginnings in Practice

When a member of my team moves on from his or her job, I tell them that I am sad for them to leave but excited for the new adventures ahead. I never beg them to come back. I never tell them how hard things are going to be without them. I never tell them that they should "know they always have an opportunity here." I don't do those things because I am bitter about them leaving—I never am. I am sad for the loss and genuinely happy for the new things God is doing in the life of that person.

I am aware of the power in my words to help a person move on or to keep them stuck. Sometimes bosses, without realizing it, plant seeds of doubt that destroy the new beginning of an employee. It is easy to feel

hurt when someone leaves your company or team, so
we say things that a person will fall back on when their
new beginning gets hard. We drop a hint that, if (and
when) things don't work out in their new endeavor they
can come back to us. Of course there are people who
mean well with those statements. They say them as an
affirmation of the person leaving, but it isn't helpful.

I've started having a final team meeting with the
person leaving and their peers. This is different than
a send-off party. It is just the immediate team, and it's
a normal meeting. We talk about normal things—and
that almost always involves things that the person won't
be a part of. It can be a little awkward, but it is important. We are moving on, and so are they. Then we share
memories.

Every team member shares one or two work memories about the person who's leaving. We reminisce.
We laugh. I affirm the person leaving and affirm how
excited we are for their new adventure. Since I work at
a religious organization, I ask the person to say a few
things and then close in prayer. And that's it. Usually
later that day or the next day we do an exit interview,
I collect company equipment, and I walk the person
out the door.

It's a standard ritual, and it has a purpose. It helps the team grieve the loss of a teammate and it helps the team member wrap up the job. That last meeting isn't just a meeting; it is an Irish wake. It gives the gift of being able to move on so we can all embrace something new.

Endings and Beginnings

When you enter into a new beginning, there are three steps you can take to grieve and "end well."

The first step is to set the last day and stick to it. This could be the day right before your new beginning or there might be a few days in between, but you need to set a last day on the calendar. If you have a hard ending already, such as leaving a job, or a hard beginning, such as getting married, this is simple—the date is already set. It gets more difficult for things that have movable dates like a lifestyle change such as diet, exercise, or any new pattern of behavior. In this case, pick a date and get others to hold you accountable to it. When we know our last day, we can prepare to grieve it.

The second step is to remember all the good things (and maybe the bad things, too). You can do this in multiple ways. You can share them with other people like I do with my teams. You can take coworkers out to dinner before you start a new job. You can share memories of your house one last time as you eat pizza on the empty floor before you move away.

Think about the Irish wake. Remember the good things that the previous season, job, or phase of life brought you. If you're alone, say them out loud (I know it seems weird, but hang with me on this). If you feel so inclined, do the same exercise with some of the bad memories, as well. If you go that route, know your context. A final dinner out with coworkers probably isn't a good time to air grievances and burn bridges. A mix of the bad with the good can bring balance to our reminiscing. The key to this remembering is to not write any of this down. Say it out loud to yourself or others, but don't put this on paper. I could encourage you to do something dramatic like burn the paper or rip it up or mail it to a friend—but you might be tempted to keep it because you just spent all that time creating a memoir of your ending. If you keep it, you might take it out later and . . . well, you know what happens then.

The third step is to cry about it. It's good to cry when we are sad or overwhelmed. When we let go of something that is ending, we need to cry sometimes. Let the tears flow. If you are one of those "I don't cry" people, I get you. I'm the same way. I'm telling you though, as a fellow non-crier, it isn't healthy. The release from crying is a physical way we can let go and deal with the emotional sadness that comes from an ending. So go ahead, give your ending a good cry so you can dry those tears and walk into a new beginning with a smile.

If you find yourself in a new beginning without having really grieved the past, it isn't too late. Set a time to have your Irish wake. Relive the good times and be mindful of the not-so-good. Cry a little bit or a lot. Say goodbye to what once was, and you can still grab hold of what is.

When you start something new, the worst thing you can do is hold onto what was. When we moved back to Phoenix, we didn't repeat the mistakes of our first trip. We grieved Wisconsin before we left; we cried with friends, went out to eat at our favorite places, and said goodbye. When we arrived in Phoenix, we dove into a new community, bought a house, and intentionally connected with new friends. It was a totally different experience, and a joyful one.

We will always cherish our memories from that time in Wisconsin, but by letting them go so they didn't contextualize our new experience, we were much happier. Holding onto the past and using it to define your present will always keep you from really taking hold of

the new things happening and the ways in which you
will encounter Jesus in those new things. It will continually rob you of joy. It will make you enter into that
new endeavor halfheartedly and, if things get really
bad, you may think with fondness about what was and
then look back. And once you look back, the results can
be irreversible (just ask Lot's wife).

2 Use What You've Learned

I got my first job when I was fourteen years old. I sold bratwurst, and I can't think of a better job for a young man in Wisconsin to have.

Every year an airplane show came to my city, attracting hundreds of thousands of people from all over the world. The week-long event provided ample opportunity for teenagers to make a few bucks before the school year started. When I was old enough, I signed up. I possessed no job skills before I started, but after that job I knew how to count back change, clean deep fryers, and sell a bratwurst. I worked at the air show every summer through high school, and it propelled me to other opportunities.

The first was work at the Harley Davidson one-hundredth–anniversary celebration in Milwaukee, Wisconsin. This was a big deal because it was a music festival, and the Rolling Stones were rumored to be the secret headliner. While the Rolling Stones were far removed from my teenage experience, I knew they were legendary and was excited to see them. At the festival I was assigned to a fry trailer right by the main stage.

A fry trailer is exactly what it sounds like. It is a small trailer filled with deep fryers, and it is a sweltering pit of despair. We served French fries and soda for sixteen hours. I managed this operation but was out of my league. My employees were all work release inmates from the correctional facility and had no desire to listen to the directions of a seventeen-year-old. It was one of the hardest days I've ever worked.

Later that year, I got a job at a tanning salon. I was fired for a mistake I made on a transaction with a customer—accidentally giving them a sale price when we weren't running a sale. I didn't mean to do that, but I did, and I lost my job. That stung.

I got a job at a gym as a personal trainer and walked with people through some really challenging experiences in their lives. People were there for various reasons. Some people needed training as they prepared for surgery or recovered from procedures. I had one client who needed to lose weight to win a bet with a friend. When he began he told me that he didn't like exercise, didn't want to diet, and wasn't going to stop drinking on the weekends. He did not win the bet.

I made copies at a place called Copy This!—a job that didn't live up to the exclamation point. I also worked at a fast food restaurant cleaning tables, in the admissions office at my college giving tours, and as a manager at a clothing store (I was robbed at that one!).

At one time, if you reviewed my resume, you would struggle to find any cohesive pattern to my work. It looked like I took jobs at any company that had a "Now Hiring" sign posted out front.

It's no wonder that my first job out of college felt like being hit by a bus. I was hired as a youth minister at a large parish and was overwhelmed in the first couple of months. I realized that my religious studies degree didn't prepare me for any of the aspects of the job other than teaching. While teaching the faith is an important part of a youth ministry job, it isn't the only part.

You need to communicate, do administrative work, and deal with unruly teenagers and upset parents. There is paperwork and information to manage and a lot of stakeholders to involve and keep track of. The days are long and exhausting. In short, my first real job was turning out to be something very different than I anticipated. Then one day our copier broke.

One of the front desk workers was frustrated, and I overheard her trying to fix the copier next to my office.

Eventually, she popped her head through my door and asked, "Do you know anything about this copy machine? It isn't working, and I need to finish making registration packets for a parent meeting tonight."

Now, I am not a handyman. I consider putting together a piece of IKEA furniture correctly a big accomplishment. I keep all of those tiny hex wrenches that come with each set, just in case I ever need one. If you ask me to do something that involves mechanical equipment, home repair, or (God forbid) plumbing, I am not your guy. But copiers? I know copiers. I used to work at a print shop named Copy This!

Within a few minutes I cleared the paper jam, replaced ink cartridges, and had the copier reset. My coworker could finish making registration packets. When I sat down at my desk, a wave of confidence hit me as a massive realization settled in: I knew more than I realized.

The clothing store taught me customer service. The tanning salon taught me attention to detail and to take ownership for mistakes. Personal training taught me how to walk with people through tough things and challenge them. That fry truck reminded me I could do difficult work with difficult people. And Copy This! gave me a ton of clerical and administrative skills, plus

I could fix our parish copy machine. I had skillsets for my new beginning the entire time. I just needed to remember.

When I reflect on my work history, I see the hand of God working. I took many of those jobs as opportunities came up or as I needed additional income during college, but in each there were skills I needed later. Your life is similar. You've picked up various skills and abilities during your lifetime. Unfortunately, our brains work the way our resumes do. We don't think about our background in terms of skills and abilities, we think about it in terms of jobs. We ask, "What jobs have I held that relate to this new thing?"

We compartmentalize work experiences and forget them when we start something new. While we should not linger on what we've left, there are skills we take with us. We walk away from a job, but the experience stays with us—at least, we need it to. Our tendency to forget where we've been is a part of the human experience.

Beginnings in Scripture

The Bible begins with the book of Genesis, but that book acts as a prequel to the big story. The principal story of God's relationship with humanity begins in Exodus with the Israelites. God made a promise to be with this group of people but they are enslaved in Egypt.

God, through a man named Moses, promises to take this group of people to a new land that will be their home, and they will be free. God, in magnificent fashion, frees the Israelites from Egyptian slavery and leads them through the desert toward this "promised land." The Israelites are excited, but after time the excitement fades. The group is wandering in the desert without provisions, and they start to complain. At one point, they even desire to return to slavery in Egypt because they are hungry and tired of wandering. The beginning of freedom was harder than the Israelites expected it to be.

The beginning turned into several years, then several more. The people wander in the wilderness for forty years before God allows them to enter the land that was promised to them. It is a new beginning. But before they enter, Moses gives them a speech. He talks through their history and the forty years in the desert. Some people in the group were born in the desert; they don't remember Egypt. Moses wants everyone to *remember* where they were before they enter into something new. If you read through this section of the Bible (it is the first several chapters of the book of Deuteronomy) you will see the word "remember" over and over. Moses doesn't want the people to forget.

Being nomads in the desert is very different than being a settled people in a homeland. Moses doesn't want the people to compartmentalize what has happened and all that God has done. He wants the people to take what they've gained in the desert with them to their new home.

In the desert, the people received the Ten Commandments and knew God in a profoundly close way. They likely formed a new language and customs (think about it—after living in Egypt, it is likely the Israelites spoke the Egyptian language). The people developed laws for a civil society and formed a community.

Being a nomad is different than living in a homeland, but what God did and what the people did cannot be forgotten because the people will need to rely on that growth as they settle. So, Moses repeats, "Remember . . . " before the group finally enters the Promised Land.

Spiritual Beginnings

When Moses gives his final speech prior to the Israelites entering the Promised Land, he focuses on the great things God has done for the people. A quick recap of God's goodness:

- God brought the people out of slavery by obliterating Pharaoh's perceived power and his army.
- God provided food out of the dew of the earth for the Israelites and, when the Israelites complained about lack of variety, God sent an abundance of quail to eat.
- God gave water out of rocks.
- God saved the people from their enemies.
- God provided a way for people to be healed of snake venom.

These are incredible events, but Moses knew it would be easy to forget God's goodness when rough times hit. So he bid his people to *remember.*

I drive my wife nuts with how I forget good things, especially affirmations and compliments. One of my "love languages" is words of affirmation, but that happens to be the love language my wife uses the least. She works hard to remember that affirming words are important to me. Unfortunately, I have a short memory. Within hours of an affirmation, I forget and will be talking about how nobody appreciates me. All it takes is one glance from her to know my short-term affirmation memory loss kicked in.

We all do this. We have an incredible family trip, but once we get back into the grind of work we feel like we never left. We spend an amazing evening with our spouse, girlfriend or boyfriend, or a group of friends, but soon after it is over we feel lonely and disconnected again. We get a great grade on a paper or finish a big work project, but quickly turn to the next assignment. We get the promotion but brush it off. We get into a graduate program and immediately start to worry.

When was the last time you really celebrated a gift or a blessing, or basked in affirmation? We often don't. Our lives are busy, and we miss the good things that happen. We need to savor those moments because that is how we remember.

Great Desserts Are Better than Deserts

The best dessert in the world is the Butterscotch Budino from Copper 48 in Gilbert, Arizona. You can argue with me on social media all you want, but you are wrong. I don't eat it often, but even as I write this I can taste it. That's because when I eat that dessert, I don't eat it fast. I savor every bite.

We need to do that with our good experiences because when we do it makes them easier to recall. Solidifying the big moments where God shows up, when God blesses us, when we receive divine affirmation, can only be done by stepping back to enjoy them.

Of course, if you are in a new beginning and standing on the edge of the Promised Land, it means the moment for celebrating in the moment has passed. Don't worry, take time to remember. Walk through God's glory in your life. Make a Moses speech.

God has been with you throughout your journey in ways you've realized as they happened and in ways you don't realize until you look back. Get out a piece of letter-size paper and some note cards. Don't have note cards on hand? Post-it notes work. No Post-it notes? Fine, rip up some pieces of paper (but promise me you will copy this over to note cards later).

Flip the piece of paper to a landscape orientation and start to draw a line. The left side of the page is when you are born, and the farthest right side of the paper is where you are now. Chart the big moments and the low moments in your life. When you are done, you will have a line drawing with peaks and valleys. Now it is time for the note cards.

Where was God in all of those moments? Find the high moments and go back to them. Think about the feelings, the people, and the experiences. Write down where you saw God present there on the note cards.

Now go through the low moments, because the Lord was present there, as well. Think of how he came through in the storms of your life. Write them on the note cards.

Now that your mind is working, are there other places where your smaller encounters with the Lord turned into big encounters? Were there "God moments" that make you say, "Wow, I had no idea what was happening right then, but God was there and it changed everything." Those aren't always moments that show up on our peaks and valleys chart. Often those small moments go unseen and happen before the mountaintop.

When you are finished, you should be feeling pretty good (after all, you've been basking in God's glory for a substantial amount of time) and have a stack of note cards. You can toss that piece of paper, but those note cards are your Moses speech.

These cards represent the spiritual evidence of how God has been with you in your journey; and, given the evidence, God is surely with you now. It is a stack of stories about how God makes all things work for good with those who love him. Take a few minutes to read through them and express gratitude for God's goodness.

These cards are going to be your fallback during your beginning. You can tape them up somewhere throughout your house or just keep them in a stack by your desk. When you start to feel like the beginning was a mistake or when you are tempted to look back at where you left, pick up a note card. When you are hitting a wall and worry you don't have the skills necessary to make the new beginning work, pick up a card. Make each card a prayer. Remember what God has done in your life and remind yourself that God is still working.

The beauty of the note cards is that they are a work in progress. You should keep adding to them. This exercise was designed to catch you up, but it isn't over. When the moments happen—the big victories, the little victories, the defeats that turn into victories, and the little moments that lead to big things—write them down. Each blessing, gift, and divine affirmation needs a card.

Beginnings in Practice

One of the best team leaders I've worked with found herself in a familiar position. Staff changes resulted in her taking new team members and areas of management. During a weekly one-on-one meeting, she expressed anxiety about the changes. I understood where she was coming from. The new department she was taking over involved different operations and goals, and it had staff members attached to it that she previously did not manage. She felt unqualified due to her lack of knowledge in this area. We spoke a bit about the transition and how I could support her, but I knew she would be successful. She had all of the skills necessary, she just needed to apply them in new ways.

Several weeks later, the new team was integrated and performing well. The team leader who took over was feeling better and told me she was continuing to learn, but felt much better about the role.

You have a toolbox of skills you've gained from past jobs. Some of those tools are rustier than others, depending on the last time you've used them, but they are still there. You will be surprised that many of your skills and talents come back to you quickly. On top of that, by applying our previous skills to new jobs we gain new toolsets while we refine the old ones. My team leader was leveraging her current skill toolbox to be successful at her job, and her success was allowing her space to learn new skills.

When we get so focused in a beginning on what we don't know or skills we don't have, we lose sight of what we do have and we falter. Our old skills can help us get started and enable us to learn new skills.

Tiny Football Players

I needed to take over my son's pee wee football team four weeks into the season. We began the year with one coach, but after a couple of directionless practices and one very miserable game, the coach and team parted ways. The other parents asked me to step in. I was volunteered by the other parents because I knew their kids' names. I've worked in ministry for more than fifteen years, and a key part of any relational interaction is learning and remembering names. I applied that knowledge to meeting my son's teammates.

This was enough of a credential for a group of parents who knew nothing about me (though I am sure they did a quick Google search) to ask me to coach the team. I was reluctant to help out because I've never coached before, and the last time I played football was my sophomore year of high school. I also wanted my son and his friends to still be able to play and that won out against my hesitation. I accepted the position via email and after hitting send I looked at my wife and said, "Well, I have no idea what I am doing."

My wife, always wise, said that I just needed to translate my skills. I had never worked with a group of kids this young; prior to coaching football, the youngest group I had worked with was eighth-graders (and that was stretching it). I didn't have the "first-grader learning style" skill, and I didn't know anything about coaching flag football.

But I had a few other useful tools.

I was organized.

I knew how to communicate with parents.

I understood how to coach other skills.

I knew how to build mentor relationships with young people.

I had a six-year-old son.

I loved football.

I was a fast and passionate learner.

These things were enough to get me started, and I'm glad that I did. I loved coaching, and the team grew tremendously. We went from losing every game to a winning season, and we got to play in the championship game. I grew, too. After coaching, I have a bunch of new tools in my skill toolbox that I'll utilize down the line. Plus, I got to have the adventure of a new beginning as a pee wee football coach.

If I had let all of the reasons I felt I was unqualified weigh me down, I would have missed the experience of a new beginning with my son as his football coach.

Skills, Skills, Skills

It's time to do a skills inventory, but you won't need note cards. We are going to make a simple resume. You aren't going to turn it in anywhere, so it doesn't need to be stylish with a professional headshot and overly complicated language to make tasks that were boring seem amazing. You can write it in a notebook, if you want. You are going back to your first job. When I did this exercise, I went all the way back to the air show. Write down skills you learned at that job. Again, don't get fancy and don't make it complicated.

In my list, I wrote:

Selling Brats at Airshow

- Customer service
- Food safety
- Cash management

Your list doesn't need to be exhaustive, especially for jobs that were a long time ago. Don't burn yourself out trying to make a simple job, like selling bratwurst, seem like it taught you the deepest lessons of life.

Keep going through your work history. Include volunteer opportunities that were substantial for you, as well. These aren't one-off volunteer moments or even mission trips. This is sustained volunteering that took place with regularity over several months. Keep writing out those skills and jobs until you have a full skills resume.

It isn't something you will turn in to apply for a job, but it is going to help you with a new beginning. This is your skills toolkit. When you are about to begin something new, go back to this document and look it over. What skills are here that you need in your new beginning? Circle them. Look at your circled skills and breathe a sigh of relief. You can do this.

Depending on the beginning, you may want to consider including some other skills in your list. If you are preparing for marriage or parenthood, skills such as customer service or inventory control may not really line up. Adding in some other soft skills may be helpful, outside of your jobs. Characteristics such as being good at listening, empathetic, and willing to take action in tough situations are all real skills that may be a part of who you are—you didn't need to learn them at a job. Remember those pieces.

We fail to leverage what we've worked hard to learn because we rationalize it away as not fitting, but that isn't true. Reclaim what you've learned and apply it.

Moses stood before the Israelites and recounted their story. It was a story about God's goodness to them, and he asked that they remember that glory. Something else probably happened, too. The people of Israel wandered out into the desert only knowing what it meant to be slaves, but God transformed them and gave them new skills and experiences in the wilderness over the next forty years. Perhaps part of Moses's speech was asking them to remember that, as well.

You can remember that, too. You will need those note cards to remind you of God's goodness and your skill resume to remind you of your toolkit. When you do that, you will be free to engage with a new beginning and take on the next critical practice: humility.

3 Ask, Listen, Watch (Repeat)

I stared blankly at the keypad and held the digital key over it again. Nothing happened. I looked around nervously and was still alone and still locked out. I tried waving the digital key over the keypad again, this time more vigorously. Nothing worked.

If you've ever needed to use a digital keypad with one of those fancy wireless key fobs, you know my pain. The idea of a wireless key system is great until you're stuck waving a tiny piece of plastic over a digital box. You will do crazy dances in front of the digital keypad to try and get that door to open, and you won't care who sees.

That was my situation. I was presenting at an event. A great group of people had invited me, along with several other people, to an amazing production studio to record talks about leadership. The production studio also had a beautiful weight room. A friend of mine organized the event, and he had access to the weight room. He gave me his key fob so I could catch a work-out in between presentations.

I was excited. When I travel, I usually end up using a hotel gym that has seven dumbbells that may or may not be in pairs and a treadmill that could fall apart at any minute. All of this equipment is in a room that can fit one and a half people in it, so if you happen to arrive when someone else is there you need to decide to squeeze in and share the space or go for a run out-side. I always pick the run outside. I don't care if I am in northern Minnesota and it's ten degrees outside, I'll take the cold over the hot breath of the other person running on the treadmill while I try to do pushups.

The prospect of using a fully stocked weight room by myself was a rare opportunity. I felt like I was Dwayne "The Rock" Johnson, filming in the morning and crushing a workout in the afternoon. I got to the door and waved the key fob, and that's where I stood for the next twenty minutes.

I waved that key fob and tapped it on the pad. I did that thing where you zoom in and zoom out with it, hoping that the movement wakes the sensor up. Noth-ing worked. I finally gave up and found my friend. "Hey," I asked him, "can you please show me why I am dumb? I cannot get this thing to work." He laughed and walked with me to the door and did indeed show me why I was dumb.

Have you ever seen those professional lanyards that hold identification cards and keys? They clip onto your shirt or belt and are retractable so when you go to pull your identification card it looks like you are about to also repel off a climbing wall. My friend's keys were on one of those. And I thought the clip was the key fob.

In one crushing movement, my friend held up his identification card—the actual key fob—to the door and was rewarded with the friendly click of the locking mechanism disengaging. I couldn't believe it. He said, "Well, there you go! Enjoy your workout!"

I was too embarrassed to tell him that for twenty minutes I kept trying to open the door with the clip that held the key instead of the actual key. As I stepped into the weight room, feeling a lot less like Dwayne Johnson, I thought to myself, "Why did I wait so long to ask for help?" No, thank you. I prefer to do things the hard way.

We've all had moments that resemble my key fob blunder. We spend hours trying to figure out how to assemble that new piece of IKEA furniture, going around and around in frustration, and when we finally ask someone they show us the step we missed and the problem is fixed in moments. We move to a school and wander around trying to find a particular building but rather than ask anyone we just get lost. We start a new job and rather than asking where we can find more pens we rummage around the supply area for thirty minutes until someone mercifully comes to save us and show us where they are hidden.

It's amazing that we do this when the solution is so simple. We know that if we go to a coworker or classmate, call the helpline, ask our spouse, or even just Google it, we could remedy the situation immediately and save ourselves a lot of time and energy. But we don't.

When we begin something new there is a reality we need to accept. Our new beginning makes us a rookie, and we don't like being a rookie. A rookie is someone who is unproven and is trying out. We've got experiences and a toolbox of skills that we bring. We are ready to crush this new beginning and think we are basically an expert already. And, therein lies the problem.

Never Take Marriage Advice from Newlyweds

If your beginning is marriage, I have an important piece of advice for you: Be cautious about marriage advice if it is coming from a couple that has been married for fewer than five years. I don't discount that there is some truth to what they are saying; all I'm saying is get a second opinion. Maybe even a third opinion.

It isn't because that couple is necessarily wrong; it's just that they are still figuring out the whole picture. My wife and I once had a couple that was married for only a few months give us advice. They thought they were experts at marriage. Maybe they were good at being newly married, but they presented their advice like they were about to celebrate their thirtieth wedding anniversary. There is danger in that mindset.

Imagine you are hiking into the wilderness. There are so many unknowns, but you want to get to the final destination—in this case, a happy marriage. Suddenly, a guide appears through the trees and says he can give you some advice because he knows how to get to the end destination. "That's great!" you say, "how far ahead have you gone?" The out-of-nowhere guide smiles wide and stands tall, while responding, "Just about forty or fifty feet!"

You wouldn't trust that guide any farther than the forty or fifty feet, and even then, what if they are going the wrong way altogether? The problem with taking advice from newlyweds (or newly anything) is that those people don't have enough experience to know definitively how their choices end up. What seems good in the first year of something may not pan out to actually have been the best practice. It may be worse in the long run.

We all want to be experts, but sometimes we don't want to wait to put in the time it takes to become experts. The reason we want to be experts is about a desire that others perceive us as being knowledgeable.

You're a Fake

When I was in my mid-twenties, I applied for a job that was my dream job. When the company called to offer me the position, I was elated. The next two weeks were a joyful blur of wrapping up the job I held at that time and preparing to move for my new role. The bliss continued in a professional honeymoon phase for another two weeks, and then one night it all came crashing down. Projects were stacking up, and I was encountering new challenges and obstacles. I started to feel overwhelmed by the work I needed to do and about how competent and put together everyone else seemed to be. The thought crossed my mind, *You don't belong here. They made a mistake when they offered you this job, and it is only a matter of time before they all find out.* Hello, imposter syndrome. It is truly terrible to meet you.

Many of us have felt this way in times of beginning. We construct a conspiracy that a series of unfortunate events have led to where we are and we don't actually deserve to be where we are. Soon we are going to be found out, and it is going to be embarrassing. This kind of thinking gets toxic very fast; it distorts every interaction we have with people and potentially destroys our new beginning. It takes what was good and makes it bad. That school you got into? They probably messed up on your transcripts. Once you fail a class they will discover the mistake and boot you out. Your promotion? Totally undeserved, and when your boss realizes it not only will you lose the promotion, you will probably lose your job. Your spouse? You somehow managed to trick that person with your charm while you dated and during your engagement, but now that you are married? Now they are going to find out the truth.

Imposter syndrome will drive you to want to be perceived as an expert. After all, if you got this far by faking it, then you need to keep faking it until you make it, right? Unfortunately, the opposite is going to happen. Instead of relying on your skills and trusting in God's providence, you will start to do weird things to seem like you are an expert. In doing so, you will become what you were fighting. There is a name for a rookie that tries to act like a veteran. We call them imposters, and they end up standing in front of a digital keypad for twenty minutes trying to open it with a lanyard.

Beginnings in Scripture

There is a remedy for imposter syndrome, and we get the prescription in one of the earliest Christian hymns. In his letter to the Philippians, St. Paul inserts a song about the humility of Jesus Christ. There is evidence that this hymn predates the letter itself by several years, putting it very close to the time of Christ's death. This hymn was sung by people who knew Jesus prior to his death and Resurrection, so the content is not theory, but descriptive.

St. Paul prefaces the hymn with the encouragement that we should "have this mind among yourselves, which was in Christ Jesus" (Phil 2:5). He then writes the song:

> Though he was in the form of God, [he] did not count equality with God a thing to be grasped, but emptied himself, taking the form of a servant, being born in the likeness of men. And being found in human form he humbled himself and became obedient unto death, even death on a cross. Therefore

> God has highly exalted him and bestowed on him
> the name which is above every name, that at the
> name of Jesus every knee should bow, in heaven
> and on earth and under the earth, and every tongue
> confess that Jesus Christ is Lord, to the glory of God
> the Father. (Phil 2:6–11)

Jesus is the Son of God, present at the moment of creation, the Word through which all the universe was created. All natural laws, universal truths, and the whole of existence were created within his presence in the Trinity. That's heavy theology.

Jesus also needed to learn how to walk, talk, read, and write. He fell down, got bumps and bruises, misspelled words, and probably hit himself with a hammer a few times as he learned carpentry. When Jesus took on human nature, while he retained his divine nature, he still needed to learn and experience humanity. Jesus was like us in every way except for sin. It was an act of humility for God the Son to subject himself to human experience because suddenly, despite knowing everything there was to know about creation as the second person of the Trinity, Jesus became a slave to the constrictions of human reality. He needed to increase "in wisdom and in stature" (Lk 2:52). He was a rookie. If

Jesus Christ, the Savior of the world and God-man, can be a rookie, you can, too.

Spiritual Beginnings

Humility is a critical virtue for discipleship and for new beginnings. As a spiritual practice, humility enables us to approach God in prayer. Humility allows us to seek forgiveness from God and from others. Humility prevents pride from tricking us into the belief that we deserve to be like God.

Humility can be practiced and developed, and if we want to grow in our faith we need to grow in humility. There are misconceptions about what humility means that we should clear up. Humility is not a lack of confidence. To the contrary, a humble person actually becomes more confident because she knows her worth is rooted in God and this worth cannot be diminished. Humility is not about being self-deprecating, but it is about being authentic. A humble person doesn't live in a lie, but is honest before God and before others.

Yet, we fear humility because we are worried it will make us look stupid or will cause us to fall behind. We don't want to humbly ask for help because we worry about how we will be perceived and that others may take advantage of what—we think—is a weakness.

I gave a presentation to a group of men, many of them older and successful, about humility. At the end, one gentleman raised his hand and kindly, but firmly, told me he disagreed with everything I said. He told me it sounded good for our personal lives, but when it came to work, humility doesn't win. If you wanted to win at work, you needed to be ruthless and tough. And I guess that is one strategy . . . if you want to stand at that keypad for twenty minutes.

Humility saves time in our faith, because instead of fighting with God, trying to convince him that we could do his job better, we submit to God's authority. We accept that God is God and we are not. We let that be enough. When we come to that place, our faith catches fire.

Humility saves time in our lives everywhere else, too, and a beginning is the perfect time to practice it.

Beginnings in Practice

Jesus, though he is humble, gives a lot of expert advice. The pages of the gospels are full of teachings that apply to us spiritually but very practically. The Sermon on the Mount, found in the Gospel of Matthew, chapters 5 and 7, has incredible wisdom. One of my favorite lines is this, "Ask, and it will be given you; seek, and you will find; knock, and it will be opened to you" (Mt 7:7). It's a great insight on prayer, and also incredibly practical.

Do you want to know something about the thing you are beginning? Ask. Looking for answers about why something you are doing isn't working? Seek them out. Trying to get a door to open? Knock (then go find your friend and ask if you are knocking correctly). It's about humility and being humble enough to ask.

We can break Jesus's words into a practical framework for growing in humility in our beginnings: *ask, seek, knock*.

Ask

Ask lots of questions. There are questions you should have frequently in your new beginning. If you are starting something new and you don't have questions, you should be concerned. If you are really digging in, there are going to be things you need to know. There is some knowledge that you do just need to gain by experience, but a lot of knowledge you can gain by asking and listening. If you don't understand a process, ask someone to explain it. If you are confused about something in a class at school, ask your professor to help you out. If you want to know what mistakes to avoid in your first year as a married couple, ask a couple that has been married for longer than five years for advice.

We spend a lot of time and energy failing in new things because we aren't humble enough to ask questions. I onboarded a new employee for a position that involved a lot of new processes for her. During my onboarding session, she asked a lot of great questions and took notes. That's right, she took notes—in a notebook! I was impressed and knew that she was off to a great start. She wasn't concerned about me second guessing whether we made the right hire. She was concerned about making her new beginning great and, can you believe it, I'm writing about her in this book because I was so impressed.

When you ask questions, you need to be prepared to listen for an answer, though. I've heard the saying, "There are no stupid questions," but the truth is there are stupid questions. We ask stupid questions when we ask a question we think we know the answer to and don't really care to listen for the real answer. Ask and, if you listen, you will receive.

I bet you already have questions about your new beginning. Pause this chapter and write them down in a journal or on some note cards. Commit to finding answers to those questions within the next two weeks.

Seek

We can approach growth in humility in one of two ways—we can wait for opportunities for humility to find us, or we can chase humility down. I've learned it is better to chase humility because I hate being caught by it. Most of us fear humbling moments, and that's why I love turning them on their head. Humbling moments don't need to be embarrassing or the result of failure. I went back to graduate school to pursue a degree in organizational leadership without any formal business education. That was a moment of me chasing humility. I actively seek out feedback from members of my team. That's me chasing humility. I invite my wife to read my rough draft and give me notes for improvement. That's me (reluctantly) chasing humility.

In your new beginning there are moments you can choose to chase humility and seek out growth. As Jesus promised, if you seek them you will find them. Ask people what you could do better, and really seek an answer (don't just settle for the "Oh, nothing! You are doing great!"). Take a class to develop skills you need for your new beginning. Ask your spouse what you've done in the first few months of marriage that is driving him or her nuts. Take the harder course in school. A lot of people avoid those conversations and situations because they might feel uncomfortable. The truth is that any expert becomes an expert by chasing humility. Some of the greatest minds in the world have learned to value failure because it brings them one step closer to success. That's chasing humility.

You probably already know what areas exist in which you should be chasing humility. I'm not going to ask you to write them all down (but you can if you want). Perhaps just write down two areas where you can actively seek humility. Go seek out those moments in the next month.

Knock

One of my favorite aspects of being a boss is when someone on my team comes by my office, and pops their head in while gently tapping on the open door, and they say, "Hey, do you have a minute to talk?"

Some people hate that. It can be a high anxiety moment that leaves people cautious. Many bosses are fearful of the "Can we talk?" knock because they fear they are about to be ambushed. I get excited because any time my team wants to communicate with me—whether it is for good news or bad news—I see it as an opportunity to build trust and for everyone to grow.

Your new beginning requires communication. Asking and seeking don't happen without communication. You've got to be humble enough to knock. I've found that most people don't because they are afraid. They don't want to be a bother, so they don't call up someone to ask the question and they don't seek out critical feedback.

I'm this way whenever I shop at a store. I will walk around forever looking for an item that a store employee could easily help me find. I just don't want to bother anybody, even if they ask me if I need help! I once walked around a Target store for fifteen minutes looking for a toy my daughter wanted. My son was with me and kept begging me to just ask an employee. Finally, one came down the aisle we were in and my son asked him. We found the toy within thirty seconds with the help of that employee. Kids have no problem with humility; they just want to grow and get the job done.

What doors do you need to knock on? Who is out there that you should be communicating with? Who needs you to stop by and say, "Hey, do you have a minute?" Line up their names with the questions you wrote down earlier. Now you have both the questions and the person or people to ask.

Rookie of the Year

Any new beginning makes us a rookie. It's just the way it is. But our rookie year doesn't need to be terrible. Embrace it. Rookies get a lot of latitude to try new things, make mistakes, ask questions, and learn. Lean into the experience as a chance to grow. Ask, seek, and knock, and you will find that you can become successful in your new beginning and, on top of that, grow as a disciple as well.

4 Create Rituals and Grab a Coffee

Jen's Java just didn't jibe. Sometimes you need to start a chapter with some solid alliteration, and sometimes you need a standard coffee spot. I moved to a new city to start a job right after college, and I was drifting. Even though I was only ninety minutes from my hometown, everything felt different. The people were a little different. The places were different. And my standard "go to work and grab some coffee" place didn't exist in this new town. I wasn't looking for a Starbucks; every town has one of those. I was looking for the hipster-vibe, single-sourced, trendy coffee shop where very serious looking people sat and worked on a new business or wrote poetry. That is the kind of place I had in my old town. I wanted something similar in my new town.

My friends recommended Jen's Java, a place they assured me was exactly what I was looking for. I went, hopeful that I was about to find my new favorite spot. When I went in, the place was deserted, except for a mom and her kids playing in the corner. I've got nothing against moms or dads being at coffee shops with their kids. As a father now, I love taking my kids out to a coffee shop and getting them a special drink (not coffee) and sitting with them. At that time, though, that wasn't what I was looking for. I was looking for a place where I could work on Saturday mornings and on afternoons when I got sick of the office and needed to be around other young professionals and hipsters who wrote poetry.

When I ordered my coffee, the person behind the counter was rude and seemed annoyed that I was in the building. I looked around confused. *Wouldn't they want some business?* I thought. *This place is dead.* On top of that, the coffee wasn't very good and they didn't have Wi-Fi, the staple of any coffee shop worthy of a Saturday morning work session. I left disappointed. Jen's Java was not going to be my new place. I walked out the front door to continue my search for a hipster coffee shop where I could work.

Setting Up (Coffee) Shop

While my endeavor to find a great coffee shop for work may seem silly, it was an important part of my move. I wasn't trying to replicate what I had back home (that would be looking backward, and we don't want to do that). I knew that a coffee shop where I could go to get out of the office and do creative work, hang out on a Saturday morning to do my personal budget, or just go be with friends was an important part of adjusting to something new for me. It was an anchor. It was going to keep me grounded in this new thing by enabling me to set up routines that would help me be successful. While I can be completely oblivious to some important things in my life, I am a fairly self-aware person. I have a reasonable understanding of my emotions and how they impact me. I know what things will help me be successful and what things set me up for failure. I recognize when I am starting to become really stressed, and I do something about it. Self-awareness is a key trait every person needs. Without self-awareness, we wind up just drifting along on emotions and reactions without ever really understanding them.

I know that I need routines and anchors in my life and that these routines and anchors are especially critical during beginnings. When we begin something, we wind up in a sea of unknowns and uncertainty. We are meeting new people, we are in new places, and we are establishing entirely new processes and behaviors. In the midst of that upheaval, it can become all too easy to lose ourselves and suddenly find ourselves out to sea.

Anchors and routines help us stay the course, even if we are charting a new course. They keep us grounded in aspects of who we are that we don't want to lose in the midst of something new.

A hipster coffee shop was that thing for me. I knew that in order to thrive I needed to have my go-to creative workplace. It doesn't matter what my job is or where I live, I need that spot. When I moved to Phoenix, I found a place called Peixoto, which became my favorite place to work. Coffee shops are one of my anchors and not just because of the delicious caffeinated drinks they brew. They ground me when things get uncertain.

We need anchors, and we need more than just one. This isn't a "well that is for some people" kind of thing—it is a human thing.

Beginnings in Scripture

Jesus, fully human and fully divine, also needed anchors. While I am not sure that Jesus sought out the equivalent of my hipster coffee shop, he did have other anchors that were important to him and that come up time and time again in the stories we have of his ministry.

Jesus was constantly grounded in prayer. It was one of his anchors. At several points in the gospels, the authors tell us that Jesus went off alone to pray. The Gospel of Luke indicates that Jesus often withdrew to lonely places in the wilderness to pray (Lk 5:16). He seemed to do this before beginnings. Prior to calling the first disciples and beginning his public ministry, Jesus was in the desert praying alone (Lk 4:1–12). Before Jesus named the twelve disciples, he went up to a mountain to pray (Mk 3:13). On the night before Jesus was crucified, he went to a garden with some friends—but once they were there he went away by himself to pray (Mt 26:36).

For Jesus, prayer was an anchor in beginnings. While you might be making one of those "well, okay, that is obvious" faces that you sometimes make when you read a book and the author writes something you feel like you could have written, I'll say this: prayer is an anchor for all of us—it is nonnegotiable. But take note of the kind of prayer that Jesus engages in as an anchor. It isn't just any prayer. He retreats and goes away alone. This is the part many people miss. Jesus has a specific anchor, not a general anchor. He isn't just praying; he is praying in solitary and deserted places (Mk 1:35). Jesus had a specific routine of prayer he followed. That's important.

The second anchor of Jesus was his time on boats and by the water. Lest you think I'm trying too hard to stick with a nautical theme, I want you to look through the gospels and note now many times Jesus is near water or boats. While none of the gospel writers ever come out and say, "Jesus was a big water guy. Loved to be out on boats," I think we can infer this. He is often with the disciples on a boat (Mt 14:13, Mk 4:35–41, Lk 5:3). He spends time near water (Mk 3:7). He even chooses to meet his disciples by the water after his resurrection (Jn 21:1–14). There is something about water that Jesus finds comforting. We can use our theological imagination to go back to the book of Genesis and remember the first words of creation that speak of waters of chaos that are formed into the sky and the seas (Gn 1:2, 6–7). This formation happens through God's Word. Jesus, as God's Word, was present at the moment of creation. Perhaps there is something about the creative power of water that Jesus found to be important and comforting. While we can muse all day about why (probably over coffee at a hipster coffee shop), I am certain that boats and water were anchors for Jesus.

Spiritual Beginnings

New beginnings provide an opportunity to discern our routines and anchors. This bears practical implications, but there are deep spiritual ones, as well. When we begin something new, our faith and relationship with God can suffer. We get so caught up in all of the new responsibilities, opportunities, challenges, and changes that we put our relationship with Christ on hold while we figure everything out. The disruption in our life can threaten established patterns of prayer and routines that help us grow spiritually, and it can be challenging to step back into them.

I've encountered this with several people during the COVID-19 pandemic. In March 2020, dioceses around the world suspended public Masses in the interest of parishioner safety. Few understood the virus well at that time, including how deadly it could be, how transmissible it was, and what, if any, efforts could be made to mitigate the spread. The best course of action, at that time, was to ask people to stay home.

For many weeks, and even months, people watched Mass online since they couldn't go in person, but something else was happening. People's routines were disrupted. What became the normal course of spiritual action on a Sunday suddenly was completely thrown off. On top of that, there are only so many live streamed Masses you can watch before you get burned out. For my family, that number was seven. About seven weeks in, we just couldn't do it anymore. My wife and I would watch occasionally, but we found other spiritual practices to engage as a family on Sunday. We needed to for the sake of our kids and our spiritual health.

When we were finally able to return to Mass, I was shocked at how few people came back. Many people believed that folks would be lining up outside the doors waiting to get into Mass like they were waiting outside of Costco for toilet paper. But that wasn't the case, at least not for our parish. I know experiences vary, but for many places, even as they opened up completely, parishioners didn't return. The routine was broken and was hard to start up again.

COVID-19 disrupted everyone's lives and was a beginning for all of us. In the midst of that, a standard spiritual routine also was disrupted. When that happens, we start to drift and it is hard to come back. I've spoken to many people who were not marginal Catholics but simply hadn't returned to Mass even when they could. It wasn't because they were anxious about attending or that they had a medical reason not to attend. They simply hadn't gotten around to it yet.

A global pandemic is, we hope, a once-in-a-lifetime event for us, but new beginnings are not. Good beginnings and bad beginnings both present a threat to our spiritual lives, especially when we fail to be specific in our spiritual disciplines and routines.

If your spiritual discipline is to simply pray daily or read from the Bible once a week, that is a good start, but it won't hold up to a new beginning. Eventually, praying daily becomes some half-hearted prayers while you lie in bed after a long day. Soon after, it becomes a thing that doesn't happen at all. Then we start to make excuses for our routines. We say things such as, "Well, I mean, I'll start praying a bit more when things aren't as busy." I hear this excuse very often from teenagers and young adults who are in the midst of busy seasons. The reasoning sounds good, even pious. "I want to really dedicate quality time to prayer, so until I can do that, I am just skipping it. I can't fit it in! And besides, God would want my best, right? When things aren't as busy, I'll get back into a spiritual rhythm."

Think about how crazy that sounds in the example of a parent and children. "I mean, I only have thirty minutes to spend with them. I know I would really want to spend a whole day with them, but I just can't right now! So, instead of spending the thirty minutes and it just not being what I want it to be totally, I am going to thumb through social media." That's insane! Children are going to take any time they can with their mom or dad, even if it is only thirty minutes. But for some reason, we think that unless we are able to have this perfect prayer experience with the Lord, we can't do it.

Specificity and routine help eliminate this objection. Let's examine our daily prayer. If we commit to a daily prayer routine of fifteen minutes of scripture reading every morning at 6:30 a.m., we have a very specific anchor and routine. We know that, regardless of the rest of our schedule, we need to block off the time from 6:30 a.m. to 6:45 a.m. every day. Nothing else goes there. It's our Bible time. It also impacts what we do the night before. If I know I need to get up at 6:15 a.m. to get some coffee, grab my Bible, and get to my prayer spot, I am going to avoid certain decisions the night before. I am going to avoid the Hulu hole of new episodes and stop watching at 10:00 p.m., rather than pushing it until midnight. Suddenly, my routine is doing more for me than just keeping me spiritually grounded, it is making me better all around.

In a new beginning, you need specific prayer routines. Don't let yourself off the hook with some general ideas. What exactly are you going to do? If you don't lay that out and stick to it, eventually you will drift and, regardless of what success you enjoy initially in your new beginning, it will be subverted by the spiritual atrophy that occurs during that same time.

Of course, what is good for us spiritually bears fruit for us practically, as well. Routines are critical for our spiritual health, but they are a requirement for succeeding in any beginning.

Beginnings in Practice

If you have a new baby, you need a system for your diaper station. This system is essential, but at times you will find it annoying. I learned this the hard way with our firstborn, Elijah. I never changed a diaper before Elijah. Even though I am the oldest in my family, I was too young to help with diaper changing duties for my sister and brother. As I got older, I never babysat and we didn't have any close family with young kids. I lived nearly thirty years before I changed a diaper!

I think I got good at it quickly. I could get a dirty diaper off without spilling anything that might be inside. I was dexterous with a wipe. I knew how to get the new diaper on so it wasn't too tight but not too loose. I was good.

I wasn't great at keeping things organized, though. In my mind, the arrangement of diapers, wipes, and other diaper accessories that my wife placed near the changing station was arbitrary. So, when I went to replace the wipes one evening I didn't think to put them in the same spot I normally found them. I put them in a completely different spot and, in the process, moved a couple of other things around, too. As it turns out, the diaper accessory arrangement is important when you wake up exhausted at 3:45 a.m. and need to change a baby. The intentional arrangement of those diaper products enables you to automatically change the diaper and get the baby and yourself back to sleep without turning on the light. That's the key. The cardinal sin of changing a diaper in the middle of the night is turning on the light. There are two reasons for this. First, it blinds you for a moment, and in those critical seconds, your baby may choose to continue to go to the bathroom without a diaper, which is a worst-case scenario. Second, the light is going to wake your baby up completely, resulting in an indeterminate time of rocking and soothing in order to finally get him back to sleep.

After my careless replenishing of the wipes, my wife and I went to bed. Hours later, she woke me up by frantically yelling, "What did you do with the wipes? Where are the wipes?" In a fog, I got up and realized that, in the 3:45 a.m. haze I was in, I didn't remember either. My wife held my son's legs up as he remained un-diapered for a dangerous amount of time. Things fell off the changing table as we searched for the wipes. In the chaos of the botched routine, my wife failed to fully wrap up the diaper and my son, as he began to kick his feet, smeared one foot solidly in his own poop. My wife, now very frustrated, whisper-yelled, "Just turn on the light!" Sheepishly, I did, and it was game over. We found the wipes but after cleaning up my son's foot and getting the diaper on him, he, my wife, and I were wide awake. An hour and a half later, we fell asleep— but my wife and I both needed to get up shortly after to head into work. It was a disaster.

I messed up the routine. While I didn't initially think that little detail of where the wipes go was important, it turned out to be supremely important. In your new beginning, the routines and the details of the routine are important. They set you up for success. When you are beginning, you first need to set your spiritual routines. After that, you need to look for the other places where you can set up routines to help you be successful. For some things, that is easy.

If you want to start a new health regimen with diet and exercise, you need a daily routine for when you will work out and for how long. You also need an exercise routine—a piece so critical that "routine" is actually in the name. Without a program, you will show up at the gym and just wander around wondering what machine to use and how much weight to use with it. Eventually, you will gravitate toward the treadmill, where you will walk for about twenty minutes while watching *Full House* because you don't know how to change the TV. Then, after feeling awkward about how sweaty you are getting while watching Danny Tanner, you will shut it off and leave, never to return. A new beginning in exercise needs a routine.

Marriage is similar, though it likely doesn't involve Danny Tanner. Many people get married but don't understand how to balance time together and time away. It is one of the most awkward parts of being married, in my opinion. I used to wonder, "So, do I need to hang out with my wife all of the time? Like, is this one big best-friend sleepover 24/7?" I would feel guilty if I wasn't spending time with my wife at home. Little did I know, she was longing for me to do something on my own. Other people face the opposite problem. They get married but continue to operate like single people. Set up routines in marriage. When is date night? When do you take alone time to work on something individually? Do you pray together daily? What about meals? Set up a routine of marriage, and you will avoid the awkward situation of oscillating between a constant sleepover and two roommates who just happen to be married.

Beginnings at a job are a bit tougher to figure out, but you can with insight from coworkers. Do you have a peer at the company with the same job? What is her daily routine? How does she manage workflow? Does your boss have any ideas for how to be successful? Ask for insight about how to set up your day. These people probably can help you figure out how to avoid traps with a better daily routine.

For me, one standard routine is that I never check email for longer than fifteen minutes in the morning. I do a quick skim of my inbox to see what I have that may be actionable right away. If it isn't, I schedule it in for later in the day. If I have a grab bag of quick response emails, I do not start going through them. Email is a trap. Responding to those dozen emails requires only three to five sentences per email, but the cost can be devastating to other tasks. For example, it might sap your creative energy right away in the day. Think about it—do you just feel exhausted after getting through email or do you enjoy a sense of accomplishment and engagement with people on the other end of those exchanges? The trap for some of us—whether we feel drained or accomplished when we hit inbox zero—is that we think that by getting through our inbox in the morning we will feel accomplished. It's like a preset to-do list. Do you know what I've noticed, though? My inbox is never satisfied. It always gets full again. So, now I do my email at the end of the day and have found I have more creative energy in the morning for big projects. This is advice I freely offer to new team members. But maybe your boss doesn't think of things like that, and that's just fine. Ask her and she will give you the insight you need to set up a new routine. Or maybe you work better a different way. It may be important to your well-being and productivity at work to respond to emails first thing in the morning. Maybe your creative energy kicks in later in the day when you don't want emails looming. The point here is to do a careful assessment of the issue.

Take a few minutes now and think about your new beginning. What routines do you need to set in place spiritually? Maybe you already have some that you just need to define. Go ahead and define them. Be specific. What are the anchors?

Now think practically. What are two or three routines you need to implement for your beginning to be successful? If you are married or getting married, make sure you run these by your fiancé or spouse first (trust me, here).

Now, for the final step. Get out your calendar and block out times for these routines. When do you pray? When will you clear out email? When is date night? If you skip this final step and say something like, "Ugh, it is too hard to get out the digital calendar that is on the phone sitting in my pocket right now and schedule this in," you will fail. You won't do it later. You will keep putting it off until you float out to sea and are off course. Make the routine now and thank yourself later.

Finally, don't worry about the routine being perfect. We are going to be able to adjust our routines and even our anchors as we go on, but we need a place to start. Once we get the routine rolling we can go back and pause, assessing where we are, where we are going, and what is and is not working. The ability to pause and assess is the next step in beginning.

5 Pause and Assess

I was cleaning out my desk and bookshelves as I set up a new home office. "Home office" is probably a generous statement. I was cleaning out a small corner of my bedroom where, if I placed my computer at just the right angle, it looked like a home office during a video conference call. I don't know how you feel about cleaning up your bookshelves, desk, and other storage areas, but I love it. My wife, on other hand, hates it—at least when I am doing it. She enjoys keeping things clean and tidy and also enjoys clearing out storage. In a way, it feels like a new beginning. The problem my wife has with me cleaning things out is that I take a long time to do it because I get distracted by what I am cleaning.

I find a book I haven't seen in a while, and I sit down to skim through it. I come across an old notebook and start to read it. Do I really need to see my notes from my graduate school Greek course? No, but what if I wrote something really important in the margins that I didn't understand then but is the perfect note for this moment in my life right now? You can see where this gets annoying for my wife. What should take me an hour to do I can easily stretch into three hours of cleaning, reviewing, engaging in nostalgia, and repeating the cycle.

On this particular day, my wife found me hunched over a single sheet of lined note paper and was about to do that deep sigh spouses make when they find their partner doing something they disapprove of, but then she saw the sheet.

She asked, "Is that a list of your goals?"

It was. I wrote the list nine years earlier when she and I first moved to Phoenix. Some goals were crossed off. I am not sure when exactly I wrote it, but I know the year and approximate timing because of some of the goals that were on the sheet. I am not sure when I stuffed it away in my desk, either, but since some goals were crossed off I must have referenced this list for a while.

We both sat looking over the full sheet of goals and realized something incredible. There were many more that we accomplished but weren't crossed off. That meant that we continued to work through those goals even after I put the sheet away. We started to cross those off as we both now sat looking at the sheet.

I say "we" there instead of "me" because the truth is I would not have been able to accomplish any of the goals on that sheet without the help of my wife, who is incredible.

One of my goals was to finish a master's degree, which I did. Another was to complete a second master's degree, and when I found the list I had just begun a new graduate program. One item was to buy a house and have kids—check. Another item was to speak in front of a group of ten thousand people or more, which I did in 2016 at World Youth Day in Poland.

As the list went on, there were many more items we accomplished together. There were also a few that I laughed at because not only did I fail to accomplish them, but I no longer had a desire to do so. One item was to learn French, Latin, and German. I mean, you can't fault me for being ambitious . . . but I don't speak any of those languages.

Then there were other things on the list that I haven't done yet, but I still want to do. One item is to get my doctorate. Another is to be debt free. A third is to take a family vacation overseas. I put the goal sheet back up where I could see it again. After all, if I was able to cross items off my list without seeing it, I think

I can make up even more ground if that list is on my desk where I encounter it daily.

Goal Setting

I worked as a personal trainer for many years and learned the importance of goal setting. Since then, the importance has been reinforced through various leadership courses, books I've read, and trainings I've attended. We've got SMART goals, big hairy audacious goals, daily goals, and stretch goals. Companies set yearly goals, bosses set performance goals, and employees set sales and production goals. On January 1, we set health and wellness goals and by Lent we forget about them and set spiritual goals instead.

Goals are important, yet many of us fail to accomplish our personal goals. In some ways, I think we enjoy the idea of setting a goal more than following through on it. Following through requires work, and that is where we get lost.

New beginnings are work because there is inertia to overcome. If you are starting to train for a marathon but haven't been running, you need to overcome the challenge of your first twenty runs. Those first runs don't feel good, and the second, third, and fourth probably feel worse than the first one did. As you begin training, you are closer to not running than you are to running a marathon. It feels easier to give in to that inertia.

That's why we need vision-based goals. A vision is a picture of the world as you would like it to be—a picture of you as you would like you to be. It's really important to note here that vision is where you start to plan your goals, but it isn't where you end them. We are going to break down goals into smaller chunks, but first we need something bigger.

I have a friend who entered a beginning with health. He started going to a group fitness gym, and when he signed up the trainer asked him what his goal was for getting healthy. My friend responded, "I want to lose forty pounds." That goal makes sense, right? My friend wanted to be healthy and knew that his health was connected to his weight. A lot of people make health goals like that. The trainer told him that wasn't a good goal.

My friend was surprised. Isn't losing weight a good thing? Plus, it can easily be broken down into smaller parts for a SMART goal. The goal weight is Specific (forty pounds), Measurable (you can track weekly progress on a scale), Attainable (he is physically able to lose the weight), Realistic (he has no physical impediments that prevent him from losing weight), and Timely (he can work with a trainer to determine a healthy and safe timeline to lose the weight).

So, why isn't this a good goal? There is no vision behind it. He wants to lose forty pounds, but will that really motivate him when he is hungry and sore from working out? Will that help him avoid the delicious burger from his favorite restaurant and choose the Green Goddess salad, which is less delicious and more embarrassing to order, instead? No, it won't. The goal doesn't say anything about his life other than that, at some point, he will be forty pounds lighter.

I invited my friend to do an obstacle course race with me. I love to do Spartan races. I think they are like giant playgrounds for adults, plus you get to race other people. I love how they test my physical ability, and I wanted to share that with my friend. He agreed and went back and told his trainer that his new goal was to run a Spartan race with me nine months later. His trainer told him that was a great goal.

It's a vision goal. When training is hard, my friend can close his eyes and imagine crossing a finish line. When the diet is tough, he can say, "How much easier will it be to work out and get faster tomorrow if I eat right, today?" And yes, in the grand scheme of things, he will likely hit his weight-loss goal, too.

In a beginning you need vision-based goals because when the work gets tough or seems to take too long, vision pulls you through.

Beginnings in Scripture

Prior to Jesus, God spoke to people through prophets. The name *prophet* comes from a Hebrew word that is perhaps best translated as "divine mouthpiece." The prophets spoke many things for God. They called out bad leaders and urged them to repent. They foretold destruction if people did not turn to God. When many people think of prophets, they think of the fiery sermons of Amos or Ezekiel, or they recall Isaiah challenging King Ahaz. But prophets also spoke hope. They reminded the people of God's kindness. They foretold the coming of the Messiah.

One particular prophet, Habakkuk (great baby name, by the way, if you need one), speaks about a vision. This is what God speaks through the prophet:

Write the vision;
> make it plain upon tablets,
> so he may run who reads it.
For still the vision awaits its time;
> it hastens to the end—it will not lie.

If it seem slow, wait for it;
  it will surely come, it will not delay. (Hb 2:2–3)

These words speak to a particular people at a particular time (the people of Israel and the threat they faced
from their enemies) but they speak to us as well. When
we set a vision, if we work toward it, it will be realized in time. We cannot get discouraged when it seems
delayed, because if the vision is true, it will come to be.

Hundreds of years later, people were struggling
with a delayed vision in the early Church. After Jesus
ascended into heaven, many people believed he would
return again very soon. The Jewish people still felt the
weight of Roman rule and hoped that Jesus would be
the one to liberate them. Many other people, prior to
Jesus, claimed to be the messiah and were political revo-
lutionaries. Their revolutions failed. Jesus was different.
The followers of Jesus saw him raised from the dead
and, after that, these same followers worked miracles in
Jesus's name. People were filled with expectation that,
any day, Jesus would return. They recalled the words
Jesus spoke about his Second Coming and waited . . .
and waited.

And then they got frustrated. The vision was
delayed. Peter addresses this concern in a letter he

wrote. In it, he encourages people to trust in the vision that, one day, Jesus will return and triumph over evil. What should they do in the meantime, though? They should live "lives of holiness and godliness" (2 Pt 3:11). There is still work to do.

Spiritual Beginnings

Beginnings give us a chance to set new routines spiritually, but we can also refocus ourselves with our spiritual goals. Before we set any goals, we need to have our spiritual priorities straight. What is our spiritual goal?

This isn't a trick question, and you already have the answer, because Jesus gave it to you. We need to "be perfect, as your heavenly Father is perfect" (Mt 5:48). Yikes. I don't know if that is a stretch goal or a big hairy audacious goal, and don't ask me how you break that down into a SMART goal. It seems impossible.

It's a vision goal, and vision goals are about who we want to be. This one is about God's vision for us. Don't get hung up on the word "perfect" here. We think of perfection as a certain look or lifestyle. We say things like, "Ugh, their house is so perfect," or "His life seems so perfect." Think about what perfection really means. To be perfect is to be without flaw, to be whole, to be lacking nothing.

This makes sense when we apply it to God. God is without flaw, whole, and lacking nothing. When we apply it to ourselves it feels unattainable. But we are wrong. In our existence, we can achieve perfection. We become perfect when we are in heaven with God because in that moment we are without flaw, made whole in God's love, and we lack nothing. When Jesus tells us to be perfect as God the Father is perfect, Jesus is calling us to be holy—fulfilled, whole, lacking nothing.

Isn't that a vision worth pursuing? Can you imagine living a life where you are content? No jealousy, fear, frustration, anger, or desire for things you don't have? I glimpse moments like that sometimes. There was a spring day with my family when we were out to eat at this restaurant, and it was amazing. The sun was shining, the food tasted incredible, my family was laughing with each other, and in that instant I thought, *Wow, I don't need anything else right now. This is perfect.* Moments later, my daughter knocked over water onto my son's coloring book and the perfection was broken, but for a moment, I had it.

Holiness is this state of divine contentment. When we talk about holy people we aren't talking about people who are perfect, but rather people who are moving toward perfection. The way they do this is by setting a vision of holiness in front of them.

When we are starting something new, we need goals, but we can't prioritize our goals until we recognize we have a singular and major goal—to be holy. That's it. Any goal that contradicts, conflicts with, or hinders that number one goal has to be discarded. It is that simple, but simple isn't always easy.

Examining Your Progress

When it comes to holiness, we always think there is more time. But what if we don't get tomorrow? When Peter is writing his letter about Jesus's apparent "delay" he recognizes this is a possibility for the people. They will start to get lazy. He wants them to live like there is no tomorrow. Holiness is for today.

At the same time, when our vision is perfection, we can easily get discouraged. We have bad days. We slide into old habits and sin. We make the wrong decisions. I yell at my kids when they spill water on each other's coloring pages.

We balance this tension with an ancient prayer called the Examen. This prayer helps us recognize areas for growth, keep our eye on our vision goal, and avoid discouragement. The Examen is a daily prayer exercise that reviews the parts of our day and where we progressed or backslid on our journey toward holiness. There are lots of ways you can do the Examen. If you've ever done an examination of conscience before the Sacrament of Reconciliation, you are familiar with one kind of Examen.

One of the simplest forms of the Examen is based around the two great commandments (Mt 22:36–40). We ask, "Where did I love God today? Where did I love my neighbor today? Where did I fail to love God today? Where did I fail to love my neighbor today?" Simple, but not easy. If we are honest with those questions, we will discover places we did well that we didn't realize we did well, and we will identify areas where we definitely need growth.

Another kind of Examen can revolve around doing God's will. We ask, "Did I respond to God's will for my life today or did I reject it?" We can do the Examen around our values. If you've identified what your personal core values are, as they align with your faith, you can ask, "Did I do a good job living out my values today or a poor job? What went right? What went wrong?"

There are three basic aspects to the Examen exercise. First, you need to allow yourself a block of time to pray and reflect. It may be helpful to journal in order to stay focused. Second, you need to be honest. This isn't a time to avoid areas where you need to grow. It also isn't a time for false humility; if you did well in a day, write that down. Remember that by recognizing the good things you've done, you recognize the power of God's grace to work those things in you. Third, the Examen needs to be actionable. This is your way of checking your progress toward your big vision goal. If you realize a pattern of getting angry at your roommates, then you need to work on that behavior. To recognize a sin or area of struggle in your life and choose to ignore it is to compound the sin. We examine our lives so we can actively engage and change them, with God's grace.

The Examen is a great daily exercise that need only take a few minutes. You may consider doing longer examinations monthly, but five to ten minutes each day can be profoundly impactful. The concept needs to apply spiritually first, but our goals can cascade. Once we have our spiritual vision goal set, we can look forward to the goals we set for our beginning.

Beginnings in Practice

One of the Spartan races I am training for currently is called an Ultra. It is a fifty-kilometer race done over terrain that often changes elevation, sometimes upward of ten thousand feet of elevation. There are sixty obstacles in the course, and it takes accomplished runners nearly nine hours to complete it. For amateurs who are well-trained, it can take between ten and twelve hours. This is one of my vision goals for health, but if I think about it all at once I can get overwhelmed. A fifty-kilometer race is longer than a marathon. The idea of running, climbing, and crawling through mud for twelve hours is daunting, but the vision of me completing the race is compelling. The key to goals in a beginning is to keep that vision intact, but to not look at the fifty steps ahead of you before that vision. That is where we get overwhelmed. Instead of looking at every step at once, we've got to look at this moment plus one.

I need a lot of little steps because they help me focus on what is in front of me. I used to think having lots of steps in between me and my vision goal would be discouraging, but I've found it empowering. There are always a bunch of little, incremental steps between you and your vision goal at a new beginning. If your vision goal is to raise well-adjusted, faithful kids who know they are loved and can love others, you've not only got a great goal but a lot of time between your beginning as a parent and realizing that goal. There are thousands of little moments and steps in between your beginning and realizing that vision.

At first you might think, *That is too overwhelming. I need to break that into big chunks.* So you do. You look at yearly goals for how you will raise your kids, but something happens during those 365 days in between goals. You start to think about the little things. You realize that in order to make your yearly goal there are a bunch of things that have to happen, but you don't have them written down. As a result, you try to keep them all in your memory, but it is too much. Now, instead of focusing on the moment at hand, you are focused on all of the steps ahead because you don't have a roadmap clearly laid out. It's like knowing your end goal is San Diego and your starting point is Chicago, but not knowing what roads to take in between. You'll get stressed.

By setting smaller, achievable goals we give ourselves a roadmap that frees us to focus on the moment we are in and achieving that small goal, while also looking ahead to the next moment (and only the next moment). If we can concern ourselves with where we are right now and how we are getting to the next step, we will become incredibly productive and less overwhelmed.

I applied this when writing this book. I can quickly feel overwhelmed at the start of a book project. There is research to do, writing to accomplish, and then editing and rewriting. When I am looking at a blank document with the cursor blinking, it's stressful. I applied the "this moment plus one" philosophy to my vision goal of a completed book. I focused on the first paragraph and how I was going to get to my next paragraph. Did you see how small I got, there? I didn't even go "first chapter." I went first paragraph. Once I started to get rolling, I went first page to next page, then first section to next section. By the time I was midway through, I went chapter to chapter. It helped me overcome my inertia. Before I started writing, it had been more than a year since I worked on a book. When I sat down at that document, my inertia was tending toward not writing a book. I needed something to get me going so I could get momentum. So do you when you are facing a new beginning.

Some beginnings are going to pull you along whether you want to go or not. If your beginning is your first child, it doesn't matter that your inertia is leaning toward not being a parent, because that baby is going to pull you into parenthood fast with mid-night feedings and diaper changes. Other beginnings, though, are going to need you to really focus on small steps toward your vision goal.

Making It Real

What is your vision goal for your beginning? Remember, whatever it is, it cannot contradict your big, life goal of holiness. That said, if you are reading this book and you've read this far, I am guessing you probably are a noble person who doesn't have a vision goal along the lines of world domination. Cast a compelling vision for yourself. Focus on feelings rather than numbers. When I began my journey of becoming healthier, my vision goal was not to run Spartan races. My vision goal was to have enough energy to keep up with my kids and be a fun, active dad. When my workouts were hard and I wanted to quit, I would imagine myself as a man in my fifties being competitive with my kids as we played sports together and laughing while we drank Gatorade at the park. I get that this is very specific, but your vision needs to be. I would think about that vision and sometimes start crying while I worked out because I wanted so badly for it to be real. Your beginning needs a vision like that; you need a vision that taps into your feelings and emotions.

Imagine the speeches people will make at your twenty-fifth wedding anniversary or even your fiftieth wedding anniversary. Think about crossing the finish line. Picture what it will be like to hold your grandchild someday. Do a thought experiment where you get the promotion. What does it feel like? That is the kind of vision goal you need. Write it down.

Now, we've got to make it real. We aren't going to focus on ten-year, five-year, or three-year goals. We aren't going any further out than a year. I hope your beginnings take you way past the ten-year mark, but unless your beginning is marriage or parenthood, there are a lot of unknowns that can tweak our goals over the course of a year. And even then, your specific goals for marriage and parenthood may change. Let's just go one year.

Break your year down into months. Do you know what a great way to do this could be? Grab some note cards. Come on, I know you keep them with this book now. Label each one with a month and line them up. Set your vision goal after the last month. Now look at the beginning. What is your major goal for that first month? Where do you need to start? It may help to write this in pencil, as you may want to go back and tweak these. Continue to do the same for each month until you get all twelve.

Here is how my friend might break things down for his Spartan race with me:

- Month 1: Accumulate ten miles of running over the course of the month
- Month 2: Run twenty miles over the course of the month
- Month 3: Run twenty miles over the course of the month plus strength train three times per week
- Month 4: Run a 5K plus strength train three times per week

You get the idea. Each month needs to have a benchmark goal that helps you get closer to your vision goal for the year. Once you get your cards set and finalized, flip them over. On the back, write out a couple of goals that help you reach the goal on the front of the card. These subgoals will help you stay focused on the moment plus one. My friend's ten-mile goal might seem crazy in that first month, until you break it down and realize that is really only one mile every three days. That is definitely manageable. He may even do more than that and beat his goal, but everyone needs a beginning point. Choose yours and add those subgoals.

Checking In

Our daily spiritual reflection is some form of the Examen, but to do a daily examination of our goals is impractical. Checking in on your goals and progress monthly, however, is much more reasonable and practical. Some goals may require a weekly check in, but most can wait a month. Every month, look at how you are doing with your goals. Do you need to make adjustments? Are the adjustments because you set your goals too high or because you didn't work the way you hoped? This monthly evaluation is a game changer for beginnings because it helps you correct course before you get too far away. Sometimes when we get into our goals we find that we need to make adjustments as we go. That's okay. We may realize that we actually could do twenty miles in that first month rather than just ten, so we adjust our goal for the next month to be double what it was. If we don't stop to evaluate our progress, we may end up sticking to goals that actually don't get us where we need to go.

This is where accountability is key. Share your goals with someone who cares about your progress. Do your monthly review with them. Ask them to keep you on track and call you out when you slip. Invite them to keep you from focusing on anything but this moment plus one. If you have a loved one who can help you, that is great. But if you can find someone who has walked this path before and maybe even accomplished some of the goals you've set already, that is even better. If you've got those goals ready to go, then the next step we take in our beginnings is to find that person. We need to find our Jedi.

6 Find Your Jedi

The Empire Strikes Back is the best Star Wars movie in the franchise. I am not taking questions, feedback, or rebuttals at this time. I am correct on this fact. We can disagree about where the other movies fall, but *The Empire Strikes Back* is the zenith of those films. It gave us the most shocking (and most misquoted line) in movie history, "No, I am your father." (Often misquoted as, "Luke, I am your father." Look it up).

The revelation of the paternal relationship between the hero, Luke Skywalker, and the villain, Darth Vader, is the major storyline of that film, but my favorite part revolves around the story line between Luke Skywalker and a Jedi named Yoda.

Next to Darth Vader, Yoda is the character from the Star Wars movies that everyone recognizes, even if they aren't very familiar with the movies themselves. Tiny, green, and some kind of strange cross between an elf, a troll, and a grumpy old man with a lot of ear hair, Yoda is an essential character in the Star Wars universe. His manner of speaking that pays no attention to grammatical context (or should I say, "no attention to grammatical context, his manner of speaking pays"), long ears, and consistent frown are iconic.

While Yoda is involved in many humorous moments in *The Empire Strikes Back*, he is far from comic relief. Yoda is Luke's teacher. Luke possesses a powerful connection to the Force, an invisible energy that connects all living things and can be utilized for good or for evil. In order for Luke to fulfill his destiny, he must harness this power, and he needs instruction. Enter Yoda, the Master Jedi.

For the uninitiated into Star Wars fandom, the Jedi are the good guys in the movies. They leverage the light side of the Force. Characters like Darth Vader use the negative energy, or dark side of the Force. Whichever side you fall on, though, one thing is certain—you need a master (for better or for worse).

Yoda guides Luke on how to be a Jedi and trains him. Without Yoda, Luke cannot become who he is meant to be. He will either fail to meet his potential or, worse, he will end up using his power for evil purposes rather than for good.

When I watch the training scenes with Yoda and Luke, I think two things: *I wish I could use the Force* and

I wish I had a Yoda. It would be amazing to have a wise, powerful, and sometimes humorous master that taught me everything I needed to know so I could fulfill my potential. When I think about it, though, there are Jedi Masters all around me—I just need to seek them out.

Will You Be My Mentor?

At the beginning of this book, I shared a bit of my experience with the beginning of becoming an executive at the ministry organization where I worked. As exciting as it was, I was also very nervous about what the role would require from me. The thing I was most nervous about was what I didn't know. There were many practical things about the role I didn't know. I had never attended a board meeting before. I didn't understand profit and loss sheets in finance. I knew that my understanding of human resources was lacking in many areas. I knew that I was a great team leader, but I didn't know how that translated into being an executive.

Rather than becoming paralyzed with the unknowns, I reached into my past experience and metaphorical skills note cards and remembered that a skill I built up during my previous jobs was an ability to find good mentors. I recalled how critical it was to find people who had been or were in the same position that I was stepping into and who were willing to share their experience, knowledge, and time with me. I knew I had to find my Yoda, and not just one, but probably an entire team.

Mentorship is a lost art in our modern culture, and that is unfortunate. There are trades where mentorship is built into the work itself. Plumbers, electricians, and carpenters work through a system of apprenticeship through mastery that involves mentorship and instruction. Sadly, outside of trade work, we don't have a great system for mentorship. If anything, white collar jobs sometimes do the opposite of mentorship. People enter companies and rather than being embraced by veterans they are actively opposed by them. New people pose a threat to status, rather than an opportunity to share experience. We've lost sight of how important and necessary mentorship is for our development.

We also feel awkward asking for help. Remember imposter syndrome? It prevents us from finding mentors, as well. We don't want to be perceived as dumb, so we Google something rather than consult someone in person. There are great people and experts online, but they can only offer generic advice that can apply to a lot of situations, not necessarily our specific situation. At worst, Google can lead us to people who aren't experts at all, but people simply pretending to be (those newlyweds have a blog filled with marriage advice). When we land on these people as mentors we wind up moving backward.

There is a wealth of knowledge out there that we could tap into, but we have a hesitation to ask for help. If we could reclaim mentorship, we would see an explosion of creativity, innovation, and growth. We need the humility to ask for it.

Beginnings in Scripture

The greatest minds, saints, activists, and change agents in history had mentors. St. John Paul II had mentors. Dr. Martin Luther King Jr. had mentors. St. Teresa of Calcutta had mentors. The mentors are footnotes in the story of these great people, but without the mentors, these people would not have achieved all that they achieved. In a new beginning the role of a mentor is critical.

St. Paul the Apostle, the great evangelist of the New Testament, had a mentor during his beginning. When St. Paul began his ministry as a Christian, people were doubtful. Paul, formerly Saul, had persecuted Christians. He was responsible for arresting several followers of Jesus and was present at the death of St. Stephen. Paul's life was turned upside down when he encountered Jesus en route to persecute more Christians. Talk about a new beginning! After his encounter with Jesus, St. Paul was unable to see, and was led to a home to rest. Anani'as, another disciple of Jesus, was called by God to go to Paul and heal him (Acts 9:10–18). Anani'as was skeptical but took Paul in anyway. While the Acts of the Apostles is not explicit about this, we can assume that Paul had a lot to learn about Jesus and what it meant to follow him. It is highly likely that Paul needed a teacher, and that teacher was Anani'as. It makes sense. How else could Paul have gone so quickly from being a persecutor of Christians to an incredible Christian evangelist? There is no doubt that Paul was gifted—he was zealous, eloquent, and a prolific writer. He was also very intelligent as a member of the Pharisees and a Roman citizen. These were all skills he brought with him into his new life as a Christian (I wonder if he wrote them on note cards). Yet, in order to make the jump quickly from Pharisee to Christian, St. Paul needed help.

We don't often think of Anani'as but without him there is no Paul. I wonder what knowledge and wisdom he willingly poured into Paul. What did Anani'as know that allowed Paul to jump years ahead in his walk of faith? It must have been profound, and Paul used it as a foundation to do great things in the name of Jesus. Anani'as could have been scared of Paul for any number of reasons—the least of which was a fear that Paul might take his job. But instead of choosing fear, Anani'as embraced Paul, and our Church grew tremendously for it.

It is evident that St. Paul continued this legacy of mentorship, pouring himself later on into Timothy as a student, encouraging him in the ministry that Timothy undertook. The words that Paul writes to Timothy, as recorded in two letters in the New Testament, are moving and powerful.

The need for mentors is not a business concept or mode of learning, it is biblical and necessary for success in life and success in our faith.

Spiritual Beginnings

Do you remember those Magic Eye posters? They were a pattern of colors and designs that didn't look like anything. However, if you looked at them the correct way (usually by making yourself go cross-eyed), a 3-D picture emerged that was there, but lay hidden beneath the design and perspective.

Our lives can be like those Magic Eyes. We may look at our circumstances and situations and see random patterns, colors, and lines. Sometimes we are so close to things in our lives that is hard to see a bigger picture. This is especially true in new beginnings. When we lack the perspective of a bigger picture, we can easily feel lost. This is where a mentor is critical.

The mentor sees the picture in the Magic Eye; they can make sense of situations and circumstances because they have an outside perspective. This perspective becomes especially important when we consider our spiritual lives.

One of the great spiritual writers, St. Ignatius of Loyola, encouraged the use of spiritual directors to help us make sense of our spiritual journey. These spiritual Jedis offer us an important perspective that we can't get on our own. For St. Ignatius, it was important for a person to have a spiritual director in order to stay accountable to their spiritual commitments and to have a person who could call out danger or trouble before it happened. He knew that as people discerned God's will for their lives as they worked toward that vision goal of being perfect, there were going to be challenges that they would not know how to navigate. This is especially true when it comes to making significant spiritual decisions.

I once had a big decision I needed to make about a job. An opportunity came up out of nowhere that would allow my family and me to move closer to my wife's parents and also make more money. It seemed like an incredible opportunity—the kind of thing that is a no-brainer to accept. It would have been an exciting new beginning. I assumed this was a done deal when I was offered the job, but something inside me still felt off. I brushed it off as simply being nervous about leaving my current job to take on something new and move across the country. I brought this up with a spiritual mentor, and his encouragement to me was to lean into my feelings of discomfort and ask why I was struggling, rather than ignore them. He told me that God may be using that to signal that the job, while good financially, may not be good for my holiness. When I did that, I realized that while the pay and the move were good things, the job itself was not something that interested me. I turned down the job and, as time wore on, it turned out to be the right decision.

The decision was difficult, but ultimately was affirmed as time pressed on. We found an incredible community in Phoenix and also discovered that prolonged periods of visits from my wife's family offered us intentional time to be with them that we would have taken for granted if we had moved close to them. We love the local school that our children attend and, though it took some time, my wife and I both readily admit that waking up to sunshine every day (even if it is over 100 degrees for about a quarter of the year) is pretty good for our mental health.

Ultimately, though, my wife and I realized that I would not have been happy in that new role if I had taken it simply for my wife to be closer to her family. While that may have been a noble thing initially, it also could have laid the groundwork for a lot of resentment later, which wouldn't have been fair to her. Furthermore, that resentment would not have been good for our overall holiness, and that is the big goal. Of course, at the time we made the decision, we didn't know any of that. We could only make the best decision for holiness in the moment and trust in God's providence.

I couldn't have made that decision without the help of a spiritual mentor. His advice to me is what differentiates a spiritual mentor from a career mentor. His main concern was my holiness. He asked the right question: "What does this mean for your walk of faith?" He saw that I was considering a job for the wrong reasons and that I needed to be pushed to think more deeply about it and to speak to my wife honestly about it. When I did, we had a difficult and honest conversation. In the course of that conversation, she shared that while she did desire to be closer to her family, we needed to step back and consider what was best for our immediate family. What would be best for our kids? What would be best for our marriage? What would be best for us? When we laid those things out on the table, we realized that a desire to move home was really about looking backward, not forward. In discerning it more deeply, we realized that moving back to Philadelphia wasn't going to be a good fit for us as a family.

Spiritual mentors are important, but not a lot of people have them. They can come either in the form of spiritual directors who have specific training in it or in mentors we have who are simply wise spiritually. A priest who is a regular confessor for us can be a great spiritual mentor. Whoever they are, the key factor is that they must be someone who is spiritually mature and who is interested in your holiness above everything else in your life. It is even better if you find someone who is inclined to take interest in other parts of your life. While that seems callous, it is important. Your spouse or best friend can't be your spiritual mentor because they have a deep interest in the whole of your life. While they are probably interested in your holiness, as well, they are going to have bias and unhelpful filters when helping you examine your spiritual life. My wife would have told me that moving closer to her family was a good thing for my holiness, and she would have really believed that. Emotions, though, can cloud our judgments. A spiritual mentor doesn't care about your career, your finances, or any other decision you make except for how it relates to your holiness.

The conversation that my spiritual mentor encouraged me to have with my wife was wise on many levels. First, I thought I knew what my wife wanted in the situation—but I hadn't really had an in-depth conversation with her about it. Second, my wife hadn't stepped out of the situation, either. She was excited about moving home, but she didn't stop to consider that there were other factors impacting the decision besides proximity to family. In a similar way, she hadn't stopped to ask, "Will moving home help me be holy?" We both needed to have that conversation, and have it together, but we were both avoiding it because we thought we knew what the other person thought.

A word of blessed caution: Any kind of mentorship requires humility, but if you find a good spiritual mentor you will grow in humility exponentially. This person is going to hold you accountable and help you see things about yourself you cannot see. This is the word of caution: if you are unable to accept that kind of support, you may not be ready for a spiritual mentor. If that is you, I will also give you a word of advice: you need a spiritual mentor. Suck it up and go find one.

Beginnings in Practice

I got into an Uber in Los Angeles after landing at LAX, which some people think is an awful airport. I disagree. If airports were comparable to the afterlife, LAX would be purgatory. You recognize that LAX is a purging experience, but it isn't the worst. You are confident you are going to end up where you need to go, and quite often the prayers of the faithful can help you make your connection on time. I don't know the theology behind that, but I am certain it is true. Chicago Midway is hell. It's a place of total despair, and grace is not efficacious there.

Ubers at LAX are an extension of purgatory, but a higher level. You are almost where you need to go, but you are still en route. You go to an entirely separate parking lot that takes about fifteen minutes by bus to get to and then you need to request your Uber and wait another ten to fifteen minutes.

I was almost out of purgatory because the Uber pulled up. I got in, and the driver looked at his phone, which displayed my destination. He nodded a few times, and then closed out of the maps app. I was confused. In every Uber I've taken the driver uses some kind of maps app so they find the best way to get me to my destination on time. This guy wasn't even loading up the default Uber app to provide directions. After we started on our trip, I got nervous. Where was this guy taking me? Does he know what he is doing? I finally asked, "Hey, so, um, you aren't going to use a map?" The guy was very kind in his response and simply said, "I've lived in LA my whole life. I know this city better than that computer does."

He was right. I kept track on my Uber app, which also laid out a suggested route and estimated time of arrival. We beat it by eight minutes. He took all kinds of routes that the map never considered that avoided traffic, stop lights, and areas with slow speed limits. As I got out, I thanked him, and he said, "I told you I know LA." I left him a significant tip.

Mentors are people who know the roads, which is why we need one in a new beginning. They can tell you where you are going to hit bumps or get stuck, and they can even give you shortcuts. A good mentor differentiates a beginning that gets off the ground quickly versus one that struggles to launch. They can save you time and energy and put you much further ahead.

Good mentors are hard to find, but they are not impossible to find. You just need to know where to look. There are two kinds of mentors—direct mentors and indirect mentors. Direct mentors are people you meet with personally, whether that is face-to-face, via videoconference, or over the phone. You know this person. You can find a direct mentor by chance or by intention. Some mentorships are organic and simply happen. Your new boss takes you under her wing. You meet another married couple through your church and hit it off, but they happen to be fifteen years ahead of you in marriage and offer you guidance. A teacher from high school stays connected with you, offering insight as your journey continues. It is amazing when it happens, and if you have people like this in your life right now, hold on to them. Don't let the relationship die. Set up monthly phone calls, coffee meetings, or Zoom get-togethers.

Not all of us are lucky enough to hold on to these kinds of organic mentorships. It is more likely that we will need to seek out mentors. This is intentional, direct mentorship. It requires more work, but the reward is greater, as well. An intentional and direct mentor is someone you ask to mentor you. Depending on the relationship, you may be able to just come out and ask, "Hey, will you be my mentor?" If you know someone already, this direct method works great. If you don't know someone well, though, you may need to take some steps. A simple first step is asking them to get together in person or via phone or video to pick their brain. This is what I did with Meagan.

Meagan is an accomplished COO with incredible insight and years of experience in operations. When I began a job as an executive, she was a person I identified who could give me some insight about my new role. I wanted to learn from her. I also barely knew her. I reached out and asked her to get together for coffee so that I could ask her some questions. She agreed, and our time grabbing coffee together helped me grow tremendously and helped us get comfortable with each other.

You may need to do that. At some point, after enough coffee Q and A sessions, you may simply come out and ask if someone will mentor you. More likely, however, the routine will grow organically so that those coffee get-togethers begin happening on a regular basis, preferably at your favorite hipster coffee spot. Suddenly, you have a mentor.

When you target a person to ask to be a mentor, there are a couple of important things you must consider. If you can filter your mentor candidates through these questions early, you will save yourself a lot of time and energy down the road.

First, the mentor must be willing to pour everything they know into you, free of charge. I don't mean free of charge as opposed to you paying them money. I mean that the mentor can't expect anything back from you— favors, loyalty, or work—in exchange for what they are giving you. This doesn't mean you won't still work with this mentor or want to do them favors or be loyal to them—a mentor may even provide opportunities for you that come in the form of work. What this means is that the mentor can't expect you to do those things. This is the humility of mentorship. You pour all you've worked so hard for into someone else and you expect nothing in return. Yoda didn't gain anything from giving Luke all he learned; in fact, it was frustrating more often than it was empowering. But Yoda saw the bigger picture and wanted Luke to be great.

The next thing a mentor needs to have is the knowledge you need. While this seems obvious, we sometimes miss this point. You need a mentor who has walked where you are about to walk. Recall our newlywed couple; while they may feel they are ready to mentor other married couples, they just haven't gone far enough. Be careful to select mentors who have actual experience to give you, not just theory.

There are also people who are great mentors, but just aren't the mentor in an arena you need. Perhaps you have an organic mentorship with that old high school teacher, but his area of expertise isn't in the field of your study. You can keep that person as a life mentor, but recognize that he isn't going to be able to be a mentor for you as you embark on a new major in school. While skills can cross over, mentorship requires a person to have played the game. While a former baseball player and coach can certainly transfer some skills to hockey, there are going to be significant gaps. Find a mentor who has walked where you are about to walk.

Finally, find a mentor who can challenge you because they care about you. A mentor wants what is good for you and is willing to fight for it, even if it means fighting against you. A spiritual mentor wants your holiness and a beginnings mentor wants you to succeed. You need to find someone who isn't afraid to tell you when you are doing something stupid or when you are making a mistake. While a good mentor will ultimately leave a decision up to you, they will also care enough to let you know the perils of particular choices before you make them. You don't need a mentor who agrees with every choice you make. Candidly, if you have a mentor who is continually affirming of your choices, you need to find a new mentor because one of two things is happening. You may be a secret genius who needs no mentorship, in which case you should start a space exploration company to rival Elon Musk's and then send me some money as a thank you for helping you realize how incredible you are. Unfortunately, the more likely situation is that your mentor isn't really paying attention and is agreeing with everything you say to make you feel good. That isn't a good mentor, that's a yes-person, and we don't need people like that in our lives.

You may have people who fit the three criteria above in your life already. If so, start asking them. Ask them to go for coffee with you. Pick their brains. Take notes. Progress the relationship. These people are essential to your beginning because they will help you get further, faster.

The Indirect Mentor

There are times when we may not have mentors who fit our filters or we can't find people who can commit to meeting regularly with us. Don't despair. While direct mentorship is preferable, we can find some indirect mentors while we grow direct mentor relationships. Our world is incredibly connected. Just a little more than ten years ago, we didn't have access to thought leaders, authors, CEOs, speakers, and influencers the way we do now through social media. This provides all of us with a unique opportunity to find indirect mentors. It is as simple as subscribing or following.

Find voices in your field who are experts and listen to them. Tweet at them. Hop into their Clubhouse and listen in, maybe even ask a question. Read their books and listen to their talks. While you won't be able to sit down and have coffee, you can still learn a great deal from these people. On top of that, you would be surprised at how often you may receive a response. If you are an expert on a topic and are active on social media, responding to questions helps build your brand. It is an opportunity to show your practical expertise.

I am surprised at how many people could take advantage of this social media access to thought leaders but simply don't do it. We still operate with a mindset that these people are inaccessible, like we need to wait in a meet-and-greet line for several hours just to get an autograph and ask a simple question. This isn't the case anymore. You can find several indirect mentors after just a few hours of searching online. While they won't be able to be directly challenging, they can say challenging things and, more important, can give you insight into how your beginning can grow into something bigger.

Finding Your Jedi

There is a whole world full of Jedi out there, you just need to find the one who can teach you. There are people, right now, who can help you grow in your new beginning. All it takes from you is some effort and embracing some awkwardness. Luke traveled to find Yoda, Yoda didn't seek out Luke. It is unlikely that your mentors are going to find you first. Go find them and grab coffee or search them out online and follow their social media. Ask good questions and get answers. A mentor is going to push you further ahead in your new beginning than you can get on your own, and that is an incredible thing.

You aren't looking back, and you've got a skills resume. You are asking good questions, finding mentors, and leaning into humility. Your new beginning has a great foundation, but there is one final piece—the secret ingredient—to making it really successful. Every new beginning needs joy.

7 Embrace Joy

"I love this class." I sat in front of my computer with a PDF of an academic article open on the screen. My wife was in our bedroom (also known as my home office) working on copyediting across from me. "That's great babe—keep that joy." I made a face. *Keep that joy?* What does that mean?

The conversation occurred during the first class of my new graduate school program. I embarked on a new beginning in pursuit of a master of science degree in organizational leadership. I was loving the program. It was accelerated coursework that allowed me to earn my degree in just over a year and, halfway through my first six-week course, I was all in. I read all the articles and even the recommended reading. I took detailed notes. I spent hours on my papers, but it seemed like minutes. I was excited for this new beginning and the opportunity to grow in a field I was passionate about.

Why would my wife encourage me to "keep that joy"? I could see how joy may fade in a two- or three- year program, but we were talking about fourteen months here. I could definitely keep my joy.

Two months later I sat at my computer, stressed out with an open Pages document, trying to write a final paper for my third course. My wife came into the room with some tea for me and asked, "How are you doing?" I took my head out of my hands and looked at her. "I'm tired," I said, weakly. "Remember, keep that joy," she said and walked off. My wife is concise and profound. I was excited about this new beginning, but my joy had faded. If I didn't find a way to reclaim that, the next few months were going to be very, very difficult.

I've Got That Joy, Joy, Joy

When we talk about joy, we need to make an important distinction. Joy is not happiness. We can be joyful and happy, for certain, but we can also be joyful and sad. We can be joyful and angry. We can be joyful and confused. We can't be happy and sad at the same time or even happy and angry (I mean, I suppose if you are, that makes you some kind of supervillain). Joy is a disposition, happiness is an emotion.

When we enter into a new beginning, joy is what holds us together. Joy allows us to embrace each moment plus one, and find good things about every circumstance. Joy sees every part of our beginnings as an opportunity to encounter Jesus in a new and profound way. That is what this book has been about—while there are practical ways to begin well, our beginnings are really about finding ways to spiritually grow. If we lack joy, however, our spiritual growth will be stunted. We won't be able to embrace our new beginnings.

It is possible to be joyful even if your beginning wasn't by choice. We've spoken of beginnings in positive terms so far, but we know that beginnings can come from hard things. The death of a loved one is a beginning. A job loss is a beginning. The end of a romantic relationship or a divorce is a beginning. We don't like those things, but beginnings don't care about whether or not we choose them. Sometimes beginnings just happen. If we can embrace every beginning with joy, we can take the good and the bad beginnings and leverage them in positive ways. Joy pushes us through when the novelty of our beginnings wears off.

Beginnings in Scripture

I love the Bible. Whenever I open up the pages of this collection of inspired writings, I encounter God in a new way. I sometimes even find God in the long and confusing codes of Old Testament law or in the winding

New Testament genealogies. But there is one passage I've always struggled with, and it is in one of Paul's letters. This particular letter may have been one of the oldest pieces of writing in the New Testament, which makes it that much more frustrating—this phrase is one of the closest to the early Christian community. St. Paul is writing to a group of people in Thessalonica, and he gives them this encouragement at the end of his letter, "Rejoice always, pray constantly" (1 Thes 5:16–17). It sounds so good. It's another one of those wooden signs you buy at a hobby store and hang in your living room. I'm a practical person, though. Rejoice always? Like, all of the time? And pray constantly? You must be kidding me. I've got things I need to do, Paul, and sometimes life isn't all that joyful.

I get cynical when I read these words, but I really should embrace this wisdom. It is possible to rejoice always, and it is necessary for our walk of faith. After all, if joy is a disposition and not an emotion, then it is possible to rejoice always. While joy is a necessary attribute for Christians at all times, it takes on a special character when we enter into a new beginning. So, what makes it so tough to be joyful?

I think the expression, "You are trying to steal my joy," is hilarious. I've only heard it used in jest, but I always laugh. I use it with my wife when she tells me the dishwasher needs to be emptied before I head to the gym. "You are just trying to steal my joy," is my reply, and her reply is, "You are trying to steal mine by not emptying this dishwasher." Fair enough. Clean dishes notwithstanding, we live in a world that often steals our joy. We read stories in our news app about tragedy and sorrow. We listen to friends engage in politically charged conversations and then not speak for weeks. We worry about our finances, our futures, and our circumstances. There are things that steal our joy.

When we start something new, there are exciting moments and challenging moments. It is easy to lean into inherently joyful moments. The first few weeks at school bring new opportunities and friendships, and that brings joy. When we get married, we work through a "honeymoon" phase where we look at our spouse and think, "Wow, I married this person. She is so amazing!" At our new job, we love how our new work corresponds to our skill set and feel like we are thriving. But a few months later, the script changes.

We feel buried under our school work and realize some of our new friends are actually super weird. We look at our spouse who is playing video games rather than emptying out the dishwasher and say, "Wow, I married this person?" We get to work and meet with our boss, who we quickly have come to dislike, and leave frustrated that he handed us a pile of work that has nothing do with our job, but that we need to get done by Friday. The joy has successfully been stolen.

Beginnings hit bumps—sometimes they start out bumpy and sometimes they get bumpy. Without joy, we will find ourselves succumbing to adversity. Joy elevates us beyond the moment because it allows us to embrace what is good in every moment. This isn't just a best practice, it is a spiritual superpower.

With Those Who Love God

While I struggle with Paul's words to the Thessalonians, there are words he wrote to the Church in Rome that I love. These are equally as worthy of a hobby store, wooden sign with white paint. "All things work for good for those who love God" (Rom 8:28, NAB). You may have seen that one before. It is an affirming scripture quote. If I love God, he makes good things happen. Great, right? Worthy of a wooden sign.

But that isn't the only translation. The *Revised Standard Version* renders a slightly different translation, which has significant implications. This is the RSV version of that same passage: "In everything God works for good *with* those who love him." Did you catch it? Instead of "for," we see "with." The Greek can be translated both ways, and both ways work, but they say something different. One of them talks about *what* God does for us, while the other talks about *how* God cooperates *with* us.

I like this second version better because it is closer to how grace works. Grace is free and undeserved favor from God—what's more, it is a share in God's divine life. We don't earn it, and we don't do anything to deserve it as reward. God just gives us it to us. Grace, however, requires cooperation. God respects our free will, and forcing something on us, even something as good as grace, would violate our free will. We need to cooperate with what God gives us. So, in all things God can work for good with those who love him. The "with" is about us.

Joy comes from cooperating with God's work in our lives and recognizing that any circumstances can be used to draw us closer to God. Step back and think about this for a moment. If you really know and under-stand that at every moment God is seeking to do some-thing incredible in your life with every circumstance, good or bad, how does that make you feel? If the really challenging moments are something that God can use for your benefit as much as the good ones, do you feel comforted by that? I certainly do. When I lean into that feeling, suddenly I experience a disposition—I feel joy.

Joy lifts me through circumstances because joy is rooted in the trust that God is making it all work for my holiness. This is why a mark of every saint that has ever lived is joy. Even despite the most challenging circumstances, they leaned into their relationship with the Lord to carry them through.

Practicing joy as a spiritual disposition happens by engaging the practices we've outlined already. Keep daily spiritual routines and make an Examen. Find a spiritual director and remember the good things God has done for you. We build up a disposition of joy when we do these things. Intentionality is key here. If you follow the spiritual practices laid out for your new beginning, joy follows.

Spiritual Beginnings

Gratitude gives birth to joy. When we take time to be grateful, joy follows. Think about the people you know who you would classify as "joyful." I bet they are people who are tremendously grateful. They are thankful for what they have in life and don't seem to really need anything beyond what they already have. These people are wonderful to be around. There is a connection between gratitude and joy.

When I think of joy, I think of my daughter. She is joy embodied. I strive to be as joyful as she is in her life. Her joy, though, really is a disposition. The normal things she does are joyful. She had a beginning during the writing of this book. She began preschool. She loves preschool. Every day she comes home and has something new to tell us about preschool. Gratitude comes naturally to my daughter, so she has never wavered on how grateful she is about what she learns.

One day, as we began our mealtime prayer, she stopped us. "No," she interrupted, "that isn't how we start prayer in school. This is how we do it." She hopped down from her chair, with a smile on her face, stood proudly, and said, "Prayer hands ready," and folded her hands in front her. Then she said, "Begin. In the name of the Father, and of the Son, and of the Holy Spirit . . ." As she sat down, she looked at me and said, "I am so happy I learn new things in preschool." Gratitude brings joy. We pray this way almost all the time now.

When we get into our new beginning, especially if it is a positive beginning, we are initially mindful of the things we are grateful for. Just as my daughter is excited to learn about prayer hands, we find things we are excited about. It comes very easy to us. We look over at our spouse and think, "God must have spent a little more time on you," and we come home from our new job singing songs like we are in a Broadway musical. When the beginning is good, it is easy to be grateful.

If our beginning resulted from something negative, though, or when the novelty of good beginnings wears off, it isn't as easy. We need to work to find areas where we can be grateful. Enter the gratitude journal.

You don't need note cards for this, but a digital journal (or an actual journal, for bonus points) is necessary. You don't need to spend more than two minutes on this each day. That is less than the time it takes to cook a Hot Pocket in the microwave.

I started a gratitude journal, and now it is part of my daily routine. I'm not a journal guy. In my mind, keeping a journal conjures up images of emotional teenagers expressing their deepest feelings in a pink book with some kind of heart shaped locket. That reference itself is deeply rooted in my '90s child upbringing, but you may relate. You might not be a journal person, either, so let my experience put your fears to rest. I write two lines, and neither is a complete sentence, every day. At the time of this writing, my beginning is school, so every day I put at least one gratitude note about school. What do I love about it? What am I grateful for? Those notes are important because they help me remember how awesome the opportunity to pursue a graduate degree is for anyone and that I get to do that right now.

When you begin something, you need a gratitude journal. Write down two things, at a minimum, that you are grateful for. Make one of those things related to your beginning. The other one can be about anything. It's a simple practice, but it can profoundly impact your overall disposition and joy. Sometimes your gratitude is going to go beyond little things, though. In the course of your beginning there are going to be wins, too. You need to do more with those than keep them in a journal.

Beginnings in Practice

There was a time when my job was very cyclical. I coordinated the production of curriculum resources for churches, and we released a new set of youth nights, training materials, and retreats every four months. The months leading up to release were tough. There were setbacks when writers didn't hit deadlines. We got into projects that turned out to be more compli-cated or lackluster than we thought they would be. We encountered difficulties with production. Even though the work was similar every four months, every set of resources produced a different experience. At the end of it all, we received printed resources at our office and, as a staff, packed them in boxes and shipped them to churches.

That process took a few hours, and afterward we all sat down and ate lunch together, shared about the resources, and celebrated as a team. We would sometimes play lawn games outside, as well. Those were great lunches.

As our customer base grew, we needed to outsource this final piece of the production process. We were shipping too many boxes to build them, pack them, and ship them from our office, so we started working with our printer to do that for us. At first, it was a relief. Finally, no more box packing days. But after a couple of months, we all noticed something. While we lost the box packing process, which few people really enjoyed, we also lost our celebration. We lost the moment that marked the completion of one big project. Instead of celebrating, we hit the "upload documents" button on our printer's website and moved on to the next thing. Not long after that, people began to drag a bit. The cycle wasn't enjoyable anymore, but nothing had changed except celebrating the win. We decided that we would bring back celebration lunches, even though we no longer packed boxes in the office. We needed to celebrate the win.

In your beginning there are going to be wins, but you will be tempted to skip over them. You will reason that they are too small to celebrate or you will be too busy to stop and enjoy them. Did you just complete your first semester of college? Great; go out to dinner with friends and celebrate. Handed in your term paper? Treat yourself to a movie. When my wife and I bought our first couch, we cooked a unique dinner at our house and ate it at a table set up by the couch. We were so excited that we purchased our first piece of furniture as a married couple that we wanted to celebrate it. Celebrating the win goes a long way toward building joy.

If we fail to stop and embrace the win, life just becomes mundane and routine. We move from one project to the next without stopping to embrace the good things God has done. Again, it is easy to do this in a positive beginning. Everything feels like a win. But once we get into the grind of school, work, marriage, parenting, or moving on from an ending, we wear out quick. Celebrating the win allows us to take a breath and embrace joy all over again.

Sometimes you can schedule the celebration of the win. When I was creating those shipments, I knew when we would need to pack boxes. It was easy to schedule in time to celebrate the win. Anniversaries, ends of classes, and project finishes are easy and appropriate times to celebrate wins. Be open to the spontaneous celebration of wins, too. When I got my contract for this book, my wife and I popped open a bottle of wine and bought the family Chick-fil-A. It wasn't a flashy celebration, but it was important for us to celebrate something good.

Have Fun

I recently introduced my kids to the Mighty Ducks movies, but not the third one, because unless Emilio Estevez is in it, that movie or show doesn't count. They loved the movies and the rest of the afternoon featured my son running around our house with a broom hitting a tennis ball yelling, "Knucklepuck!" It was awesome.

At one point in the first Mighty Ducks movie, Coach Gordon Bombay, played by the irreplaceable Emilio Estevez, realizes that hockey isn't just about winning. Hockey is about having fun. He tosses a bunch of beach balls out on the ice and the Mighty Ducks all realize the goodness of sport. It's heartwarming.

If you want to embrace joy in a new beginning, it is important to be grateful and it is important to celebrate wins, but it is critical to have fun. Beginnings can be fun. You meet new people, experience new things, and learn new skills. While that can also be daunting, it is only as anxiety-inducing as we let it be. Even when our new beginning isn't positive, we can embrace what is fun about it. I'll admit this is tougher, and you probably aren't going to start there. I don't know anyone who was laid off from a job and forced into a new beginning that thought, *Wow! Filing for unemployment and wondering how I am going to provide for my family sure is fun! What a delightful new beginning this is. Huzzah!* Consequently, I don't know anyone who routinely uses the word "Huzzah," and I feel like that is a hole I need to patch in my friend network. Sometimes beginnings aren't fun at first. If you can redirect the negative into a positive, though, fun can start and joy will follow.

It's All about Prayer

"Rejoice always." While it seems like a tall order, if we recognize that joy is a disposition it suddenly becomes attainable. Gratitude, celebrating wins, and remembering to have fun help us strengthen this disposition. Joy makes new beginnings more than possible, it makes them shine.

We can't forget the second half of St. Paul's encouragement, though: "pray constantly." Your new beginning can become an opportunity for constant prayer and incredible spiritual growth. When our guard is down in a new beginning, Jesus can work in our lives in ways that previously were unavailable. When we begin anew, we can see things about ourselves that need to change. In a new beginning, we can evaluate our routines and recommit to a new spiritual path. Every beginning is an opportunity.

We've moved beyond the past, and we aren't looking back, but we are taking the skills we learned with us. We are asking the right questions and listening so we can grow, always rooted in humility. We've got our coffee shop (or whatever other anchor and routine you need), and we are making sure to set vision goals and evaluate them. We know who we need to be our Jedi, and through it all we know to embrace joy.

We've got what we need to not simply begin something new, but to make it a spiritual experience that will bear fruit beyond the new beginning, to take us beyond it and into something far greater and far more eternal. Every story has a beginning, and we start new stories all the time. Jesus is going to do something new through you.

Prayer hands ready? Begin.

Epilogue

You never outgrow beginnings, and that is what makes life such an adventure. Beginnings come in every size and form—from the big beginnings of jobs, marriages, babies, and big moves to the little beginning that is every new day—you are going to experience beginnings until the day you die. And even then, something new is happening. As morbid as it may seem, death is a beginning in itself as we enter into the fullness of eternal life.

As you move forward in whatever beginning, fresh start, next step, or life-changing opportunity you are about to encounter, I want you to remember this powerful statement: you are infinite. Of all the beginnings you will experience, you only had one true beginning. There was one definitive moment when you came into existence, and that moment was intentionally willed by God, who breathed life into you. That was your first beginning of many beginnings, but you have no end. You go on forever because your soul is eternal, and God desires desperately to draw you back to himself for all eternity. The choice to enter into that life is yours.

My sincere hope is that, through the preceding pages, you've learned how to begin well. I love seeing people flourish in new beginnings. There is something so adventurous and wild about someone finally taking a step into the unknown to do something new. I love helping people succeed in their beginnings. But if this book was just about being successful in the short-term, then I missed an opportunity. I don't merely want you to succeed at all of the new beginnings you experience, I want you to encounter Jesus Christ—the God who loves you—through each of them.

There was a period of my life when every morning I woke up and simply said, "Jesus, I love you." It was the first thing I said. I can't say that is a practice I've maintained consistently. It wasn't that I was an extraordinary saint in that moment, but I think I had a very ordered understanding of my world. At the most foundational level, I woke up (a new beginning) and recognized Jesus there. I was alive, and alive is good. I had a new chance to encounter the Lord in a profound way and to live an adventure. What else could I do but express my love for the one who gave me breath?

I wish I could say I still did that, but some days it is hard. I wake up filled with anxiety and concern. My alarm goes off on my phone, and instead of thinking of Jesus I start combing through my notifications (a tragic side effect of having teammates who live on the other side of the country and start their day three hours ahead of me). I begin working, and rather than seeing the opportunity that the beginning of a new day affords me to know and love Jesus more intentionally, I see another day at the grind. I think there are many of us like that. We get caught in a cycle and rhythm of life that numbs us to the work God is continually doing in us and around us.

Beginnings shake us out of that numbness, whether we want them to or not. It is in that shaking that we can suddenly see Jesus again, in a new way, and fall in love all over again. We can approach the start of something new and say, "I love you, Jesus," as we take those steps. It is that relationship with Jesus that sustains us through every beginning—whether born from new opportunity or tragedy—and also carries us through our last earthly ending, in death, and into the beginning of eternal life. In a way, every beginning is really about preparing our hearts for that eternal beginning.

I don't know what adventures await you, but I know that Jesus will be with you in them. I don't know what led you to this book, but I do believe that God had a hand in it, because this new beginning is a place that Jesus wants to meet you and show you something new.

So don't look back. Remember the skills you've learned along the way. Find mentors and coffee shops. Live joyfully and embrace the adventure. No matter what your new beginning looks like, I know this: Your heart will race with excitement and anxiety, and your feet may feel heavy as you step forward. You will look ahead and know that when this new beginning reaches its end you will be different. You have no idea how that is going to happen, but you do know that life is going to change. It will seem scary, but you will step forward and Jesus will step forward with you as you enter into a new adventure and find something new about who you are and who God is. The adventure awaits; now go, and begin well.

Joel Stepanek is the vice president of parish services at Life Teen International where he guides teams that support Catholic parishes in creating and sustaining vibrant youth ministries. He is an internationally sought-after speaker and the author or coauthor of a number of books, including *Chasing Humility*, *True North*, *The Greatest Job on Earth*, and *The 99*. He also is a contributing writer for The Youth Cartel and Youth Specialities.

Stepanek earned a master's degree in religious education with an emphasis in youth and young adult ministry from Fordham University and a master's degree in organizational leadership from Colorado State University. He has served as an adjunct faculty member at Franciscan University of Steubenville.

He and his wife, Colleen, live in Gilbert, Arizona, with their children.

joelstepanek.com

Twitter: @ChasingHumility

Instagram: @ChasingHumility